ROUTLEDGE LIBRARY EDITIONS:
ECONOMICS AND SOCIETY

Volume 7

THE COMING OF THE WELFARE STATE

THE COMING OF THE WELFARE STATE

GERTRUDE WILLIAMS

Routledge
Taylor & Francis Group
LONDON AND NEW YORK

First published in 1967 by George Allen & Unwin Ltd.

This edition first published in 2026
by Routledge
4 Park Square, Milton Park, Abingdon, Oxon OX14 4RN

and by Routledge
605 Third Avenue, New York, NY 10158

Routledge is an imprint of the Taylor & Francis Group, an informa business

British Library Cataloguing in Publication Data
A catalogue record for this book is available from the British Library

ISBN: 978-1-032-97576-4 (Set)
ISBN: 978-1-041-12916-5 (Volume 7) (hbk)
ISBN: 978-1-041-12920-2 (Volume 7) (pbk)
ISBN: 978-1-003-66724-7 (Volume 7) (ebk)

DOI: 10.4324/9781003667247

Publisher's Note
The publisher has gone to great lengths to ensure the quality of this reprint but points out that some imperfections in the original copies may be apparent.

THE COMING OF THE WELFARE STATE

BY
GERTRUDE WILLIAMS
(PROFESSOR LADY WILLIAMS, C.B.E.)
Professor Emeritus of Social Economics in the University of London

London
GEORGE ALLEN AND UNWIN LTD
RUSKIN HOUSE MUSEUM STREET

LADY WILLIAMS has acted as independent member of many Wage Councils; was member of a Committee on occupational diseases and is now a member of the National Youth Employment Council and of the Central Training Council.

She has lectured widely and is author of *The State and the Standard of Living, The Price of Social Security, Apprenticeship in Europe, Economics of Everyday Life,* etc.

ACKNOWLEDGEMENTS

The author and publishers gratefully acknowledge the help of the following in the provision of pictures: The Governors of Guy's Hospital, Fig. 22, The Inner London Education Authority, Figs. 19 (two photos), 20, 21, Radio Times Hulton Picture Library, Figs. 1–3, 8, 9, 12, 15–18.

FIRST PUBLISHED IN 1967

FILMSET BY KEYSPOOLS LTD, GOLBORNE, LANCASHIRE and
PRINTED IN GREAT BRITAIN
in 11 point Plantin type
BY JARROLD AND SONS, NORWICH

CONTENTS

1. THE CONTRAST BETWEEN 1890 AND TODAY

What is the Welfare State? As this book is about the way in which it came into being it seems sensible to get some idea of what we are talking about. But, unfortunately, that is not so easy. There is no universally accepted definition of the term and, indeed, it is probable that most people who might be asked what they understood by it would find themselves in difficulties. We are not even sure who first coined the term. It began to be used by a few people during the thirties and by the end of the Second World War, it suddenly seemed well established in ordinary conversation.

In a general way the term refers to the many methods by which the State, through a host of different services, tries to raise the standard of living of the population and help people to meet the various troubles through which most of us have to pass at one time or another in our lives. Practically all these services (though not quite all, as will be shown later) have come into existence during the present century and a contrast drawn between the position of most members in the community in the late nineteenth century and today gives some idea of their importance.

As it was

Suppose we take 1890 as our starting point and see the way in which a man met his responsibilities then, and compare this with the situation today. In 1890 the ordinary working man was expected to provide for himself and his family in all circumstances and to make arrangements for any periods when he might not be able to work. How he did it was a matter for himself to decide. The work he got, the wages he was paid, the conditions under which he worked, the provision he made for old age, or for unemployment or for the times when he could not work on account of sickness or accident, all these were considered to be entirely his individual responsibility. He was expected to save part of his earnings when he was in work in order to have enough to fall back on at other times.

If he could not meet these obligations he had only two alternatives before him. First, he could appeal to charity, either the generosity of some person to whom he was known or to a charitable institution founded by generous people to help those in distress. Second, if he were absolutely destitute, and that means that he had not enough means to buy himself and his family the barest essentials of life, he could apply for poor relief from the local Board of Guardians. As can be seen from this second alternative, the State did not carry its principles so far as to be ready to let people die in the streets of starvation; but unless a man's misfortunes reached that desperate limit he had to bear them as best he could. The

1. *A Sunderland slum about 1890*

State did, indeed, accept certain responsibilities; it set up schools to which parents were compelled to send their children to be educated up to the age of 11, and it made some modest regulations about the hours and conditions of employment of women and children, but its supervision did not penetrate further than the fringe of life.

As it is now

The contrast with the situation today is overwhelming. It is still true that a man has a legal obligation to provide for himself and his dependants (i.e. his wife and young children) and the work he undertakes for this purpose is a matter of his own choice. Again, the wages he gets are settled by negotiations between his trade union and the employers' association; the State has no part in this, not even in enforcing the agreement when it has been made. But though both the choice and the responsibility are his own there is a whole network of institutions to help him. Instead of having to tramp mile after weary mile, as he used to, until he saw a factory wall with a 'Hands wanted' notice pinned to it, he goes to the local Employment Office maintained by the Ministry of Labour. There he can get information about all the different kinds of work available, not only in his own area, but all over the country. If the job is away from home he can, in certain cases, receive financial assistance to pay for his travelling expenses and his lodgings until he can find a new home.

Long before he becomes an adult attached to a particular industry he can get help in choosing the kind of work on which he is going to rely for his future livelihood. The Youth Employment Service employs officials to help young people to find out much more than they possibly could from their own narrow experience or that of their parents, which occupations offer the kind of job that is suited to their tastes and aptitudes. This service begins whilst the children are still at school and have time to think about the future and it continues for the first few years of employment in case they wish or find it necessary to alter their first choice.

Although the majority of wage-earners belong to trade unions which can protect them by negotiating their pay and conditions of work there are many millions who do not. In earlier times these unorganized workers were almost always the worst off. They were too poor and ignorant to protect themselves and had to take whatever pay was offered as the only alternative was starvation. This meant that the closer they were to destitution the lower the pay they got because they were too frightened to stand out for a higher wage. Nowadays this has changed. The Government sets up Wages Councils to give unorganized workers something of the same sort of protection that the unions provide for their members. These Councils have statutory powers to fix minimum rates of pay and employ inspectors to see that no employer pays his workers less than these rates.

It is, however, in other matters than wages that the greatest

2. *Seeking work at the London docks in 1887*
   (1) *Distribution of penny breakfast tickets*
   (2) *The rush for work at the dock gates—the foreman selecting labourers for the day*
   (3) *Unloading a ship—the lucky few at work.*

changes are to be found. One can say with some truth that now there is hardly any sphere without some legislation designed to raise standards of living or to provide for the welfare of members of the community throughout the whole of their lives. One part of this assistance takes the form of direct money payments which supplement earnings or which replace them when the individual is not earning. The other part is in the form of services which are given free of charge to the individual and are paid for out of rates and taxes. The following short summary gives some idea of the extent of this help.

Help in cash

Wages are paid for the job done and can take no account of the number of children the worker has to keep on them. Since 1946, however, family allowances are paid out of national funds to parents of dependent children up to the age of 16 or later if they are having full time education. The majority of workers do not receive payment when they are not working and everybody is liable to have certain times when they cannot work. This may be due to unemployment in the trade to which he belongs or to sickness or an accident or age, for most people hope to go on living even when they are too old for regular work and can retire. In all these cases, whether the earnings are interrupted, as with periods of unemployment or sickness, or whether they cease altogether by retirement, a minimum income is now assured through the systems of national insurance and retirement pensions. This kind of income is a statutory right payable by law under prescribed conditions and is fixed on a national scale; but people have all sorts of individual problems that do not always fit exactly into legally prescribed definitions so there is, in addition, a right to ask for National Assistance. This takes into account all the circumstances of the person making the application; it is not a fixed weekly amount, like the insurance benefit, but varies according to need and may be paid above the insurance benefit or retirement pension.

Help in kind

Family allowances and insurance and retirement benefits are examples of the first kind of state help mentioned above; the others, which are given in kind rather than money, are much more numerous. School meals are provided at much below cost price and milk is provided free for schoolchildren; local authorities build well-equipped houses for which tenants pay considerably less than the economic rent, mothers of young children are given special foods free of charge. Children who do not receive proper care from their families—either because they are orphaned or because their parents are unable or unwilling to look after them—are taken into care by the local authorities and new homes are found for them until their own families are able to look after them again. There are special homes and schools for the mentally sick and physically handicapped where they can be helped to overcome their disabilities as far as possible and homes for the permanent care of old people or others who are in need and have no normal family to care for them.

Everybody in the community has the right to free medical attention and to the hospital and other services prescribed by his doctor. Education is free not only up to the age at which it is legally permissible to leave school but up to a later age if the pupils and their parents are willing for them to continue. And for those willing and able to go on to higher education there are money allowances to pay for board and lodging, books and other necessary expenses.

The change in the climate of opinion

All this is a far cry from the situation described in 1890. And it is this help given by the community to its members in many different ways that we mean when we speak of the Welfare State. This change has not come about of itself. It is the result of the work done by thousands of people who felt compassion for the sufferings of their fellow citizens or who believed it to be wrong that men should have to bear ills that could be remedied. It has not taken place all at once nor was it planned from the outset as a comprehensive scheme. Big social changes never are. People have had to learn, bit by bit, by many experiments how to bring about the improvements they thought desirable. Very often the schemes they tried did not prove as successful as they hoped or they brought with them other unwelcome consequences that could not have been foreseen. And every change has demanded an enormous amount of thought and argument and discussion. We have to remember that human beings are not machines that can be taken apart and put together again to form any pattern that happens to please us. We are born into families which are part of a particular community and we grow up with ideas and attitudes of mind that are usual in that community.

We take it for granted, for example, that a child who is brought up in England speaks English and one brought up in Italy speaks Italian. In fact, we can often tell not only the country but the district from which a person comes—Cockney, or Yorkshire or Somerset and so on. This seems quite natural to us; but, of course, it is not natural except in the sense that it is expected. It is part of the way human beings develop and learn to be adult. And what is often overlooked because it is not so obvious as speech is that, just as a child learns to speak in the way that is customary in the locality in which he lives, he also picks up all the other ways of behaving in regard to food, manners, religion, ideals, customs, morality, beliefs of what is right and wrong and so on. By the time a man is adult he is accustomed to think along certain lines—to look at the world through particular spectacles, as it were, and it is not at all easy to change this way of looking at things.

Every group of human beings has accepted ways of conduct which regulate the behaviour of members to one another and to the outside world. In a school, for instance, there are not only the rules made by the headmaster or headmistress which must be obeyed, but one soon learns that there are certain things which are 'not done' and others which are. They are simply the customs of the school. Sometimes these change quite quickly just as fashions in dress do; but sometimes they go on for so long that they become established traditions which most pupils would not dream of breaking. The same thing happens in society as a whole. There are laws which cannot be transgressed without incurring a stated punishment and there are established customs and traditions which the majority obey because they do not want to be criticized by their fellow members of society. Most of these are taken as much for granted as the capacity to speak one's native language and are often considered equally 'natural', so that any idea of change is sure to meet with a great deal of opposition because it involves changes in the ideas and attitudes of mind with which people have grown up.

This book deals with the radical changes that have taken place in the minds of the community with regard, in particular, to the relationship between individual and communal responsibility for maintaining and improving the standards of living of the mass of the population. Some part of this change of opinion has been due to the influence of men with the intellectual power to think of things afresh, to look at the world with new eyes and thus to open men's minds to new ideas. But much more is due to the fact that we are continually faced by serious problems which we have to try and solve as best we may. Often enough, our solutions are 'opportunist', that is, they are not the result of some carefully thought out theory of how problems should be dealt with; they are the efforts of men with limited knowledge who are aware of some suffering which they think they can try to alleviate. Then perhaps we find that an improvised way of coping with a difficult situation can be improved upon and used in a more general way and so what we had earlier looked upon as a revolutionary break in our customary way of dealing with life's problems comes to be taken for granted as part of the ordinary course of events. This is a never-ending process; it is going on today for we are constantly faced with new situations and difficulties for which some solution must be found. But each generation begins from a new standpoint because it has grown up in different conditions from the one preceding it, with different assumptions of what is 'natural' and 'ordinary' and with different ideas of what to expect from life.

2. SOCIAL PROBLEMS OF AN INDUSTRIAL SOCIETY

(i) The working man's Britain in the eighteenth century

In the last chapter I contrasted the position of those people who find themselves in difficulties now with that of similar people at the end of the last century. Yet after all, the problems with which we all have to deal—old age, sickness, the burden of bringing up and educating a large family, the misery of mental and physical handicap—these are not new things. As long as there have been human beings at all there have always been those who were too young to provide for themselves or too old, or who suffered from a disability which prevented them from making provision for their own needs. Who looked after such people before?—and why should there have been this remarkable revolution in the ways of caring for them? To answer these questions we must know something of the profound economic changes that took place during the nineteenth century and of the social consequences that accompanied them.

Until the end of the eighteenth century life was very much simpler than it is today. There were no steamships or trains (and, of course, no aircraft) and even the roads were so few in number and so badly made that they became almost impassable in winter. The journey from Manchester to London by the 'flying coach' (too expensive for any but the rich) took $4\frac{1}{2}$ days and transport of heavy goods was quite impossible. Not only was travel difficult because of mud and broken surfaces but dangerous on account of highwaymen and footpads, and few would venture to go any distance, particularly if carrying anything of value, without an escort able to defend them.

In such circumstances people were very much more cut off from one another than they are today and this meant that each small neighbourhood had to depend on itself for all the everyday things it needed to carry on its life. Most families provided the chief necessities of life for themselves. They grew their own food, spun and wove the linen and woollen fabrics for clothes and household equipment, kept a pig and a cow for meat and dairy produce and relied on the few village craftsmen—the blacksmith, the thatcher and the tanner, for example—for the jobs that required special skills. For the little luxuries or the bits of finery they had to wait for the travelling packman who went from village to village, or for the infrequent fairs at the nearest market town, itself no larger than would now be considered a fair sized village. London, Bristol and Norwich were the only towns of any size; and the vast majority of the population—which was no more than 9 million in 1800—were born, worked, lived and died, without moving more than a few miles from the same parish.

There was only one industry of any size. The fine pastures of the British Isles allowed large flocks of sheep to be reared and for centuries already before the eighteenth century woollen cloth had become famous and was exported to many countries. How important wool was thought to be as the basis of our wealth can be seen from the fact that to this day, the Lord Chancellor sits on the Woolsack in the House of Lords.

But although woollen cloth was exported in large quantities it was not produced in factories and workshops as it is today. The rich clothiers, with capital enough to finance such a trade, bought the raw materials from the farmers and gave it out to people to work in their own homes on simple hand tools—the women as spinners and the men as weavers. Few of those workers depended entirely on the wages they got for these jobs for, as they were done at home, they formed only one part of the household income, most of which derived from agriculture. It was rare for a cottager to have no piece of land on which to grow his vegetables or to keep his poultry and most had more than this. Farms at that time were not compact and hedged as they are now but the village consisted of great arable fields divided into strips which were owned and worked by many people. Most of those who lived in the village owned some of these strips—though, of course, the number varied from one man to another—and this ownership entitled them also to put a number of sheep and cattle to graze on the common pastures.

Farming was inefficient and not very productive, for little was yet known of the science of cultivation. The strips were too narrow for good ploughing and the strips belonging to one man were so scattered that much time was wasted going from one to the other. A keen farmer could not keep his strips clean, for the seeds from his neighbour's weeds did not respect boundaries. The feed was inadequate for the number of animals put into the fields and good breeding was impossible when all fed together indiscriminately. Winter feed was difficult to get so that a large proportion of the stock had to be slaughtered at the beginning of the winter and salted down to be kept to provide rather sparse meals until the grass began to grow again. So life was hard for most people; standards of living were low, food was often scarce and there was hardly any variety. But on the whole one could be fairly

3. *A weaver's cottage in Huddersfield. The unusually large windows gave light for the hand-looms.*

sure of basic essentials and in a neighbourhood where the same families had lived for generations there were usually kinsfolk and neighbours to help over a crisis.

The 'Industrial Revolution'

The great change in this way of life came with the rapid development of knowledge and its application to productive techniques which took place during the end of the eighteenth century and the beginning of the nineteenth century. This is the period that is often referred to as the 'Industrial Revolution' but the word 'revolution' has a very different meaning here from the one we usually give it when we are thinking of a political upheaval. When we speak, for instance, of the French Revolution or of the Russian Revolution, we are referring to a sudden and far-reaching change in political life which took place in a particular year. For example, we can say that the Russian Revolution took place in 1917 for it was then that the Czarist regime was brought forcibly to an end and the Soviet Communist state was founded. But the Industrial Revolution did not take place in any particular year and there was no special event to which we can point as being of paramount importance in its development. Owing to the fact that a large number of scientific developments were taking place at about the same time and were helping and supplementing each other, the changes in the methods we use for producing the goods and services we need for our life, were so profound that people living in 1850 seemed to be inhabiting a completely different world from that of 1750.

At the present time we seem to be on the brink of all sorts of exciting new knowledge about the other planets in space. Mars and the moon have been photographed, men have walked in space thousands of miles above the earth and it is likely that soon the first human foot will step on to the surface of the moon. Suppose that these efforts to conquer space lead to the discovery of other inhabited planets and that, as time goes on, we are able to establish trading relationships with these people. There is no doubt that this would lead to enormous changes in the things we make and the resources at our disposal. But revolutionary as such changes would be we should not be able to point to any particular moment of time or any particular event as the beginning of it all. It is in this sense that we speak of the Industrial Revolution, because the application of new scientific knowledge to methods of production brought about profound changes in our ways of living.

More efficient methods of agriculture were not possible as long as the open field system existed, for no improvement could be introduced unless every individual involved agreed; so the introduction of new methods was preceded by enclosure. This meant that the owners of strips in the open fields gave them up, as also the accompanying rights to put their sheep and cattle on the common pastures, and in return received a compact holding which had to be fenced. This undoubtedly led to more economical farming and allowed experiment both in the arable and stockbreeding parts of the work; but for many small farmers it spelled ruin. Their strips were so few that the farms they got in return could not support a family and were hardly worth cultivating especially as the cost of fencing was very high. They were forced to leave the land and seek work in the towns. At the same time the new machines invented for use in the textile industry and the chemical knowledge applied to mining and the use of iron completely changed industrial techniques, for the new machines soon came to be power driven, first by water power, later by steam. This took production out of the home and into the factory for it was only when a large number of machines were housed together that it was economical to produce the power to run them. But perhaps most important of all was the revolution in transport. The discovery of methods of making a good road surface that could withstand heavy traffic even after rain, the building of a network of canals and later of railways, these together provided the most potent factor in changing the life of the people; for this enabled districts to specialize in producing the goods most suitable to their natural resources and the skill of the inhabitants, in the knowledge that food and raw materials could be carried to them from other areas and their own products be moved to the most rewarding markets.

The result of all this was that wealth rapidly increased and standards of living rose. As England was the first country to establish machine industry the markets of the world were open to her exports without any fear of competition. As she became the 'workshop of the world' she found it much more economical to concentrate more and more on manufacture and shipping and buy her food and raw materials from other countries. In consequence our food became very much more varied and less dependent on the seasons. Other countries' harvest times were not the same as ours so food was available from somewhere throughout the year; and many foods that could not be grown in England could be bought cheaply with British manufactures and transported easily in British ships. Thus, for example, tea, which had been drunk only by the very rich became the standard 'cup that cheers' for even modest households, and sugar from the colonies became a staple article of food. Meat, which had been eaten by most people only on rare occasions, became a normal part of the diet, partly because the new scientific cultivation allowed home-bred sheep and cattle to be kept alive during the winter (instead of killed and salted) and partly because better

4. *Hyde Park Corner, London, at the end of the eighteenth century.*

communications enabled them to be imported from abroad.

Clothing, too, changed, for the cotton industry was the one that developed most rapidly and extensively with mechanization. Although all the raw cotton had to be imported the large supplies of coal and iron close to Liverpool, the port of entry, enabled cotton cloths to be produced at low cost and, as cotton materials can be washed more easily than woollen, the substitution of cotton for much of our clothing improved health by raising standards of cleanliness and personal hygiene. Towns also could be more easily cleaned when road surfaces were improved and the use of iron pipes instead of wooden ones for water and drainage allowed supplies of piped water to be available for larger numbers of households and sewerage to be removed instead of remaining in the streets to breed disease.

With more food and healthier conditions the population increased rapidly. For hundreds of years prior to the eighteenth century the population had risen so slowly that the change was hardly perceptible to those living at any one time but between 1750 and 1830 it doubled itself. Not only did it increase so spectacularly but it was also redistributed. The big centres of population had been mainly in the southern half of England gathered round London, the metropolis and centre of Government and fashion, and Bristol and East Anglia, the big wool producing areas. But with the development of machine industry, the coalfields became the new big urban regions. Every machine industry depended on supplies of coal and iron and as these are both heavy and bulky things to transport it was generally easier to carry the raw materials needed in production to the coalfield instead of the other way round. The big coalfields were mainly in the Midlands, the north-west, and Scotland and it was therefore these areas that became the richest and the most highly populated.

The social results

All this development brought about profound changes in the lives of the mass of working people.

(1) It created a large wage-earning class which was a new phenomenon. There had, of course, been many people who depended on getting a job for pay in order to maintain themselves; but only a small minority depended on this and nothing else. As I have said, most had at least a bit of land on which to grow part of their food so that even when paid work was difficult to get they need not starve. But the growth of the factory system based on the use of water and steam power and the consequent development of large urban areas brought about a sharp distinction between agriculture and industry. The man who earned his living in a factory in a town had no land to help eke out his earnings and was too far removed from the country to be able to get seasonal employment on a farm if his industrial employment failed him.

(2) There came also to be a clear distinction between the breadwinner and his dependants. In both agriculture and domestic industry (that is, when spinning and weaving, for example, were done at home with simple hand tools) all the family worked to produce the income on which they all lived. Even the younger children could help on the farm and in the simpler industrial operations; but when industry moved out of the home and into the factory this was not so easy. Factories required the worker to stay at work for 10 hours or more a day; and the wife could not leave the young children uncared for during so long a period. So it became more and more usual for her to give up paid employment after marriage whereas before she had made a big contribution to the upkeep of the family. And although at first very young children were employed in the factories and mines the gradual realization of the burden imposed on them by long hours of work led to legislation prohibiting them from such employments while they were below a certain age. So the same circumstances which led to wages becoming the sole source of livelihood had also the effect of creating the 'dependant family'. The wife and young children ceased to contribute to the family income and became entirely dependent on what the husband and father could earn. This change did not come about all at once and, indeed, in the cotton industry it remained usual for large num-

bers of married women to be employed in the mills. When the textile industry first left the homes for the factories, it seemed natural to employers to take on women because they had for so long been traditionally associated with this occupation; but this was not true of the newer industries, particularly engineering and metal which soon began to rival textiles as the dominant industries of the country, nor of building and furniture making which expanded enormously as a result of the upward surge of population and by the end of the last century only about one in ten of married women worked for pay.

(3) The new methods of production were much more efficient than the old but they had in them an element of risk that the others did not have. The small farmer, who grew food for the needs of his own family or for sale in a nearby market town, and the worker, making shoes or furniture or cloth for his neighbours, could not produce very much in a week; but unless there was some natural calamity, such as a harvest failure or serious cattle disease, he was fairly sure of his living. The man who depended on the wages he earned in a factory or a mine had no such sense of security. The demand for his labour was affected by a whole series of circumstances over which he had no control. The failure of the cotton crops in America might throw thousands of men in England out of employment; or the invention of a new machine might make a skill, which had taken years to perfect, a drug on the market. Storms at sea might delay raw materials from getting to the factory or the finished products from reaching their market. Changes in national boundaries, with their effects on the incidence of tariffs, might completely alter the demands for the goods the industry was geared to make. All this meant that just at the time when the majority of people came to depend solely on their wages for their livelihood and that of their families, the element of risk came to be much more pronounced than it had been.

The development of easy means of communication led to an increase in personal mobility. The enclosure of farms forced many people out of the villages and the new industries were mostly located on the coalfields. Hundreds of thousands of men moved to new areas in search of work and wages and this movement broke up the old pattern of social life. When generation after generation remained in the same village there was almost always somebody to help if one found oneself in trouble. If the mother of a family fell sick there was usually a sister or aunt or grandmother living near enough to help with the household. But when a man went into the towns he did not take all his sisters and cousins and aunts with him and if he was in trouble he was among strangers. He had neither kin nor familiar neighbours to whom to turn for help. As time went on new social patterns were developed in the towns but it takes a long time for people to get accustomed to strangers when for centuries they have known everybody living near them and have known their background and families as well. Think now, for example, how difficult it often is for people who move to new housing estates or to the New Towns to feel as friendly and 'at home' as they did before they moved; and people today are very much more accustomed to moving from place to place than were those who first staffed the new industries. But although so many thousands moved to areas where they were unknown the assumption continued to persist that everybody always had some member of his family to whom to look for help in time of distress.

(ii) The destitute

Every human community must make some provision for those who are too young or too old or too ill to provide for their own needs. How this provision is made depends on the code of morals or the religion or the philosophy on which that particular community is founded. In nineteenth century England the dominant set of ideas was known as '*laissez faire*' or individualism. Put very briefly, this expressed the view that every man was the best judge of his own happiness and must be left free to make his own choices of how this might be achieved without interference or dictation from anybody else. But it followed from this that he must also be prepared to suffer whatever consequences might ensue from his choice. The State had to arrange for the general framework of law and order, but apart from that it must stand aside and let each man order his life as he pleased and face the results whatever they might be. There was a general belief that it was only by making men realize that they could not look to others for assistance if things did not turn out as well as they had hoped that there would be sufficient incentive for them to choose wisely and use their initiative and ability to the utmost. If people knew that they could look for help from others they would not trouble to develop their skills or try to

5. *February 1868, the 'labour yard' of the Bethnal Green Employment Association.*

Owing to the 'exceptional suffering among the poor . . . a large part of the population, at the best of times, is on the verge of pauperism . . . a great effort has been made recently to prevent these persons and their families from sinking into the hopeless ranks of chronic pauperism . . . The Association endeavours to avoid degrading the industrious poor by any direct alms-giving, all relief being given in return for work'—from the Illustrated London News. *These men are breaking granite for the roads.*

find where work was available or work hard enough to keep a job when they had found it. In this view of society there were only two justifiable alternatives to starvation if a man was unable to make ends meet.

Help from the community, and its limits

(1) Public assistance could be provided out of funds raised by local rates for those who, after investigation, were proved to be destitute. The State was not prepared to take its beliefs to their extreme logical conclusion and let its citizens die in the streets but they had to get very near this limit before help was forthcoming. A family might have to sell or pawn all its belongings before it could be considered destitute and even then, the assistance that was forthcoming had to be deterrent in character; that is, it had to be of such a nature that people would not apply for it unless they were really desperate. This 'deterrence' was achieved by insisting that an able-bodied man could not be given help unless he went into the workhouse, where the conditions were extremely grim, and the

6. *A sewing class in 1868, Commercial Road, East London. Another instance of charity. The women were paid ninepence for a day's work.*

financial help given to the wife and family left outside was barely enough to keep body and soul together.

To have a member of your family in the workhouse was considered such a terrible disgrace and the means tests or investigations into the family resources were usually so harshly carried out that most people did make the most desperate efforts not to apply for Public Assistance.

(2) The other acceptable way of escape was through charity which sometimes came to the help of those in distress. Christianity taught that men are brothers and that people should give to those poorer than themselves. Fortunately, there were very many people who took this duty seriously. In some cases they set up institutions to take care of the orphaned and aged; in others they gave their personal services and money to help individuals living near them. But, of course, such help was very uncertain; it depended on whether you happened to live near to a charitable person and this ruled out help for the hundreds of thousands who flocked into the towns where nobody knew them and there was nobody to whom they could appeal.

Self-help and its limits

Most people make great efforts to meet the obligations that society puts on them and the working men and women of the nineteenth century were no exception. Faced as they were with difficulties that had been unknown in earlier periods they gradually established new ways of coping with their problems, and new types of institution were established for this purpose. The first of these were the Friendly Societies which attempted to build up collective funds to provide for individual times of crisis. It was all very well for authority to argue that every man knew that he was liable to periods during which it would be impossible for him to earn and that therefore he could be expected to save out of his earnings to provide for them. Most people hoped to live to old age, and they might expect that, in the natural course of events, they would have some sickness, so each wage earner should put aside a proportion of his wages to provide for such emergencies. The difficulty that was not fully realized was that earnings were so small that even small savings involved great sacrifices; the troubles were in the future and uncertain, for nobody knows how long he will live and men do not have exactly the same amount of illness to provide for, so to put aside part of one's meagre wages to provide for an emergency that might never occur meant starving one's children now for a possible event later on. But whilst it was impossible for any individual to know how many weeks of sickness he might suffer, any large group of men could be fairly certain that a *proportion* of them would be unable to earn each year from this cause. If each contributed to a common fund out of which those who were unfortunate enough to be ill could draw a weekly benefit the burden of such collective saving would be much less than the amount that each would have to save for himself. This was the theory on which the Friendly Societies were founded and they did an immense amount of good. A man who was fortunate enough to remain healthy might pay in for years without drawing out a shilling but he got from the society a feeling of security—the knowledge that if he did, in fact, fall ill there would be funds available for him without recourse to the dreaded Poor Law Guardians. How strong was the feeling for self help and how eager men were to make provision for themselves can be seen from the enormous number of members of the various Friendly Societies during the last century.

Unhappily a great deal of the sacrifices made by working people for these purposes was wasted for the problems proved too big for them to cope with. If you are going to build up an adequate collective fund you must know fairly accurately what proportion of people are likely to incur the risk. For example, most people who own houses today insure them against fire (this is exactly the same principle as that of the Friendly Societies). We now have records going back over many years which show how many houses do, in fact, on average get burned each year, so the fire insurance companies can calculate how much each person must pay as a premium in order to collect sufficient to meet all the claims of those whose houses are destroyed. But in the mid-nineteenth century there were no such records of sickness. Everybody knew of course that people did fall ill but nobody had any idea how many weeks a year a man was likely to be off work for this reason so the premiums had to be based on guess work. As wages were low and any premium at all involved a real sacrifice it is not surprising that the guesses were usually on the optimistic side, with the result that if a good number of members of the society happened to fall ill at the same time the society collapsed for lack of funds and men who had made great sacrifices for years to cover their risk found themselves destitute through no fault of their own.

Most people do not insure themselves against a risk unless they believe it is likely to occur so the Friendly Societies naturally attracted a large number of older men who saw themselves as likely to benefit rather than the young and healthy; and this meant again that the claims were often more numerous than the funds could meet.

Even the most successful societies could not do more than provide help for their own members and the only ones who could afford the premiums were those in fairly regular employment. This left out all those whose work was so intermittent that they dare not pledge themselves to make regular payments and it left out too the millions of wives and children who were not earners and who could not make any payment at all. And even those with generally settled work were subject to periods of unemployment—because of the greater element of risk in industry making for world markets—and might be unable to keep up their weekly payments for so long that it was impossible for them to make up arrears when they got back into a job again.

The trade unions

The second big institution developed by working people to help themselves was the trade union. According to the individualist theory the bargain between a worker and his employer was a contract between two equally free and independent adults each of which was capable of guarding his own interests. In fact, however, it did not work out that way for a worker who was, perhaps, one of hundreds employed by the firm did not stand on equal terms with the employer. The employer did not depend on any single worker to get the job done whereas the worker did very certainly depend on getting the job. If one man tried to stand out for the wage and conditions he thought right he could be fairly sure that some other worker, who had been out of work for some time and was nearer to destitution, would take it rather than starve or be forced to ask for Public Assistance. But if all the workers banded together and spoke with one voice the situation was quite different for the employer had to reckon with the fact that, unless he came to terms with them, he

7. The Yorkshire Mineworker's Association stages a gala in Barnsley (photograph about 1930)

would get no workers at all and his overhead charges would be piling up with no output to pay for them.

The strength of a trade union depended on how far it included all those who were capable of doing the job and their loyalty in keeping to the terms that had been negotiated on their behalf. It can easily be understood, therefore, that a man who had been out of a job for some time—either through illness or because work was slack—might be tempted to undercut his fellow members and take a job at low rates of pay in order to get back into employment. It was to guard against such possibilities that the trade unions began to undertake some of the same functions as those of the friendly societies. The weekly membership subscription was calculated so as to provide, in addition to the costs of administration, a fund from which those unable to earn could receive a weekly benefit to tide them over their difficulties. The types of risk insured against in this way varied from one union to another and depended mainly on the average earnings of the members and the amounts they could afford to pay weekly. The majority provided for sickness and unemployment and some, in addition, offered a modest old age pension for those too old to continue in work.

In their friendly society functions the trade unions were generally a good deal more successful than the ordinary Friendly Societies. The fact that the members joined together primarily for industrial reasons as well as for insurance against sickness and so on gave a great amount of stability to both sides of the work. The members combined because they were all doing similar types of work and not because they expected to be ill so there were not as many 'bad risks' as in the Friendly Societies; and the chance to claim help in times of need made it worth while to continue membership of the union even when nothing spectacular was happening in the field of wage bargaining. But good as this work was it covered only a tiny fraction of the working population. Building a trade union was a difficult and uphill task and it appealed primarily to the highly skilled craftsman. Even by the end of last century there were no more than 2 million workers organized in unions and the large masses of semi-skilled and unskilled workers were almost entirely untouched by them.

(iii) Public opinion changes

What happened to make people change their minds about the danger of society providing for those in need? From the outset there had been small groups who refused to accept the basic principles of Individualism. Quite early in the nineteenth century, for example, Robert Owen, one of the most successful and most famous of the new industrial mill owners, had argued that men could not possibly learn to use their abilities to the full nor practise the civic virtues if the environment were unsuitable. To prove the importance of good conditions he provided good housing for his workpeople, schools for their children and many other amenities that were far in advance of his times. There were also small pockets of socialists who argued that competitive self-interest was an immoral foundation for society and that everybody would

8. *Keir Hardie, 1855–1915. British Labour Leader*

benefit if it were replaced by collective co-operation. There were also spokesmen from amongst the workers themselves who could speak from their own experience of the degrading conditions in which so many were compelled to work and live, and of the unspeakable miseries they endured when unemployment or illness cut off their only income. Keir Hardie and men like him denounced the system on moral grounds and by their vivid descriptions of the poverty and sufferings of their fellow workers they tried to make men question the accepted beliefs.

But beyond all else, however, strange as it may seem, it was the growth of knowledge and, in particular, of accurate statistics that did more than anything else to change the whole trend of opinion.

The facts become known

We are now so used to the publications of Government Committees of Enquiry, trade statistics, annual reports of various ministries showing the conditions in the sphere of the community with which they are concerned, Gallup Polls, radio and TV documentary programmes, etc., etc., that it is difficult for us to realize how scanty was the knowledge of everybody—whether a Government official or a private person—of what was actually happening around them. There are still large areas of our life in which we make guesses and assumptions because of the lack of accurate information; but we do now have regular and accurate records of, for example, the average earnings in different occupations, the numbers of people unemployed in various industries and how long their unemployment lasts, the numbers in the various age groups, the birth and death rates, the amount of sickness in various occupations, the number of houses built and so on. So that now before we make any statement we can check its truth against a lot of evidence. But for the greater part of the nineteenth century this was not possible and consequently a large part of the beliefs that people held were based simply on guesses and assumptions of what was going on and why.

For example, during the first half of the century it was obvious that there were many more young children about than there had been before and people jumped to the conclusion that the masses of the population were having more children and that this was due to the irresponsibility of parents who trusted to luck that the parish would look after them if they could not support themselves. It took decades of careful recording of births and deaths to realize that this was quite untrue. The birth rate had not increased at all, but, owing to cleaner towns, piped water, better sewage disposal and improved medical knowledge the death rate of young children had decreased very greatly so that a much larger proportion of those born lived to run about and be visible.

In the same way it had been taken for granted that in a country whose industry was expanding so rapidly any man who really wanted a job could get one and that, therefore, unemployment was a sign of indolence or bad conduct or unwillingness to learn a trade. In these circumstances the most popular remedy for the poverty caused by unemployment was the establishment of Labour Colonies to which unemployed men could be sent to be rehabilitated and taught to be better citizens. This belief was blown sky high when the trade unions began to keep records of their members who applied to them—through their voluntary insurance schemes—for out-of-work benefit. The unions had to keep careful accounts of the men who received benefit for their rules generally restricted the number of weeks in any one year that it could be claimed and from these accounting records two important facts emerged. First, even though the number of men 'on the books' remained the same over a period, a scrutiny of the names on the lists showed that they were not the same individuals for two weeks running. Most men were in work for the greater part of the time but might be unemployed for a few weeks whilst searching for a job. This made nonsense of the 'character diagnosis' unless one were prepared to believe that a hardworking, self-respecting man suddenly became a loafer for a short time and then got his good character back again. The second fact that came to light from the records was that the total amount of unemployment varied in a fairly regular way. In some industries the variation was seasonal; for example, clothing and building, and the proportion of men unable to get work showed a regular change from month to month each year. But more important than this was a cycle of unemployment and employment that affected all industries at about the same time and showed a periodic rhythm which took between 7 to 10 years to complete itself.

It was these facts that made thinking men realize that unemployed men were not anti-social beings but the victims of circumstances beyond their control. It was the growing complexity in the structure of industry that was the villain of the piece and it was both cruel and ineffective to try, by harsh treatment, to whip men back to work when there were no jobs for them to go into.

The trade union records were only one element in the body of knowledge that was beginning to accumulate. Many Government enquiries into the conditions of factories and mines brought to light the shocking conditions and long hours of work that were the lot of hundreds of thousands in the expanding industries and gave conclusive evidence that the theory that adult workers would never agree to terms of employment that were not in their own interest was not borne out by the facts. But the most important enquiry of all that did more than any other to throw light on the nature of the new world was carried out by a private individual and his collaborators—Charles Booth, a Liverpool shipowner with a serious concern for the welfare of the common man. In a series of seventeen volumes called *The Life and Labour of the People of London* published between 1886 and 1903 he gave the world the results of a comprehensive detailed investigation, made by painstaking personal enquiry, into the actual conditions of life of thousands of people living in the working class areas of London—the industries in which they were employed and the wages they earned, the sizes of families, the rents they paid for their accommodation and what they got for it, the habits of life and social conditions.

The cumulative effect of this compilation of facts was to explode forever the general assumptions both about the level of well-being of the mass of the population and about the causes of the misery that was known to exist. Before this it had been assumed that poverty was confined to a small section of the population and that this was mostly due to their own improvidence, intemperance and reckless early marriages. Booth's survey showed this bland assumption to be completely false. Instead of finding that poverty was the lot of only a tiny section, his figures showed that no less than 35·2% of the working class population in the richest city in the world were living in absolute poverty; 12·4% classified as living in a state of chronic want and 22·8% as living under a constant struggle to make ends meet and without sufficient resources to buy the bare necessaries of life. The analysis of causes was even more startling. Bad habits such as drink and improvidence did, it is true, play some part but they accounted for only 13% of the poverty. A larger amount, 19%, could be attributed to sickness and similar factors; but by far the largest part was due to the low pay received by the breadwinner of the family. Booth calculated that 68% of poverty was directly due to low wages and the irregularity of employment.

These revelations proved so devastating that many people argued that London must be a special case and that one could not believe that similar conditions would be found in other parts of the country. But an enquiry made by Seebohm Rowntree in 1899 in York soon killed this optimism. For in York, which was not an international port like London, nor a metropolis likely to attract the derelicts from other regions, but an old settled country town with a few well established industries, more or less the same situation was found to exist; and there was no escape from the conclusion that these surveys painted a picture that was probably general in its main characteristics.

As a consequence of all this new knowledge it was no longer possible for thinking men and women to hold on to the old beliefs in all their rigidity. This does not mean that opinions underwent a revolutionary change within a few years. Few people are as rational as that would suggest. It takes a long time for new ideas to seep through a whole community and men cling to their old convictions in the teeth of endless evidence that they have no foundation in truth. But it does mean that gradually there came to be more readiness to accept that there might be occasions in which it would be right for the community to organize help for those in distress without the fear of undermining the spirit of independence. There continued to be strong and influential bodies of opinion that opposed any action on the ground that it would inevitably lead to disaster—economic, social and moral—but they came to be a smaller proportion of the community.

The working man in politics

There were two other factors which contributed to this development. The first was that more people were entitled to vote for Parliament. Until the middle of the second half of the nineteenth century the mass of the population had no vote in electing members of Parliament; but in 1867 the industrial working man and in 1888 the agricultural worker became part of the electorate and as a result both the traditional parties, the Liberals and the Conservatives, had to take some account of the needs of working people when fashioning their political programmes. Thus the whole question of 'The Condition of the People' came to be, what it has since remained, one of the liveliest parts of political controversy.

This led eventually to the organization of a party specially concerned with the interests of the mass of working men and women. In the early years they were content to work to support the election of working men as members of Parliament owing allegiance to the Liberal party as the one most likely to understand their point of view. But very soon many men began to believe that it was illogical to support the Liberal party, which consisted mainly of industrialists, when it was these very same men who, as their employers, were responsible for the bad working conditions they were trying to improve. This led to the establishment of a separate party—first the Independent Labour Party and later the Labour Party, pledged to a programme of reforms of working class living conditions. For a long time the Labour Party was very small but its effect was enormous; for it brought these matters right into the forefront of the programmes of both other parties and from that time on, these matters, which were of such importance to the lives of the masses of the community, could not any longer be ignored.

The change in men's thinking

The second factor was the effect of familiarity. As long as it was accepted that it was courting disaster to pass laws to improve the conditions of working men any proposal could be

9. *A Labour Party demonstration, Crewe, 1926 (at the time of the General Strike)*

met with entrenched opposition. But when gradually some slight experiments were attempted and it was found that the results were not as terrible as had been foretold, it was very much easier to take a further step. Bit by bit as one problem after another was investigated people began to realize that the problems to be dealt with were not simply those of a minority living on the edge of the abyss, but that the extreme poverty which nearly always came with old age, the bad housing conditions and lack of educational opportunity that stunted the physical and mental growth of the new generation, these were the conditions that coloured the lives, not of a submerged tenth, but of the general mass of society. 'The problem of preventing poverty,' said R. H. Tawney in 1913, 'is not primarily to assist individuals who are exceptionally unfortunate. It is to make the normal conditions under which masses of men work and live such that they may lead a healthy, independent and self-respecting life when they are *not* exceptionally unfortunate.'

This was the really big change in ideas; the realization that the normal conditions of life required something more than individual effort and determination. This changed men's conception of the State so that they came to demand that organized society should do for its members what they are unable either as separate individuals or as members of voluntary associations to do for themselves, i.e. to obtain such security in their standards of living as would enable them to have freedom and capacity to develop their full potentialities. The idea that certain conditions were intolerable in a civilized community came to be part of the political and psychological atmosphere and gained support for legislative proposals that twenty or thirty years earlier would have been opposed as revolutionary and suicidal.

3. THE FOUNDATIONS OF THE WELFARE STATE

(i) The public conscience—factories, towns and schools

By the end of the nineteenth century there was already a considerable amount of legislation dealing with economic and social conditions but in almost all cases it was not directed primarily at the welfare of the individual in distress, but was concerned either with the conditions of employment of categories of persons who were thought to be particularly helpless or was designed for the general protection of society.

When the cotton factories were first industrialized they relied greatly on child labour, partly because this could be got for very low wages and partly because small fingers were specially adept for some of the processes involved. Many of these children were drawn from pauper families who had become destitute and were therefore under the control of the Overseers of the Poor. According to the Elizabethan Poor Law, which was passed in 1601 and remained in force right up to 1834, it was the duty of the Overseers of the Poor to 'set to work and to put out as apprentices' the children of all those who were unable to maintain them. As the upkeep of paupers was a direct charge on the local rates the Overseers were not too careful about the types of work to which these children were put. They became domestic drudges, or were hired out as chimney sweeps or to small shopkeepers who were prepared to give them a pittance in return for the work that could be got out of them. The new factories proved a godsend to those anxious to rid themselves of the cost of supporting these unfortunate children and thousands were sent to work in these industries. Although they were called apprentices they were not taught a craft but were employed on routine jobs for intolerably long hours, and were lodged and fed by their employers in crowded apprentice houses.

The gradual regulation of industry

The exploitation of children was no new thing; they had always been expected to take their share in the work of the household and though, no doubt, natural affection generally limited the demands made on them by their parents, it is certain that in innumerable families they were expected to do an amount of heavy work that would now be considered positively cruel. But factory work brought them together in large numbers where their employment could easily be seen and so stir the conscience and compassion of those who came into contact with them for the first time. It was, in fact, a large employer of such children—Sir Robert Peel—who introduced the first Factory Act for their protection. The Act, which was passed in 1802, was not very effective for it was not yet realized that legislation is never operative unless

10. *A 'house of correction' where 'needy and miserable persons' were housed and given work. A late eighteenth-century engraving*

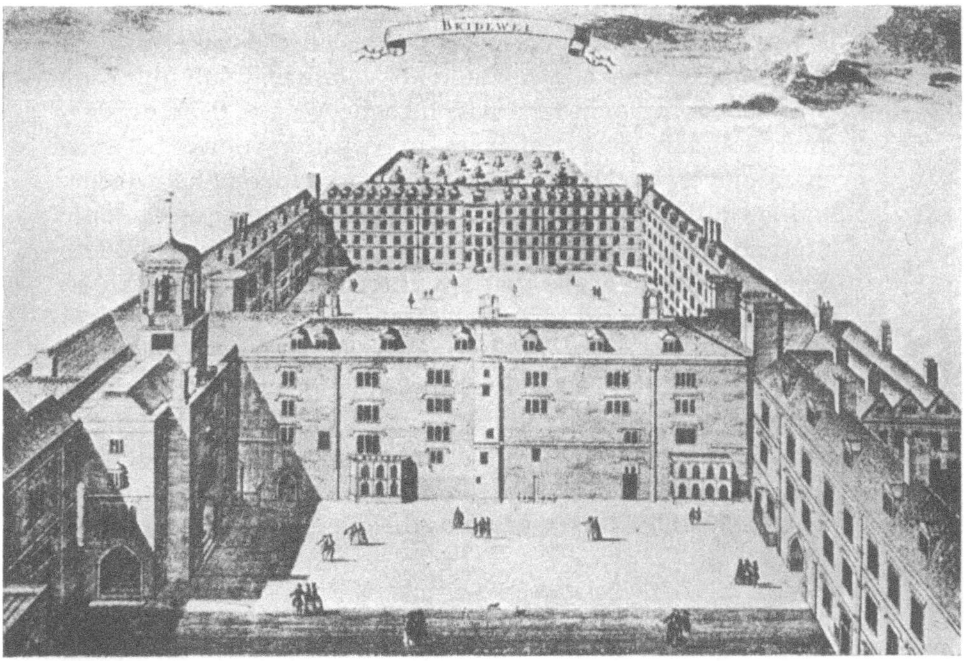

careful arrangements are made for inspection and sanctions; and it was not until 1833 that the first effective factory act, which provided for inspectors, was put on the Statute Book. By that time the pauper apprentices were no longer the principal source of child labour for the low wages earned by working men had compelled them to send their children into the factories to supplement their fathers' incomes, and the original laws which had been justified on the grounds that the State was in the position of the pauper children's parents, now covered ordinary children who had been sent into employment by their own parents.

The first factory laws dealt only with cotton mills for it was believed that the bad conditions and long hours of work of which the outside world had suddenly become aware were confined to the newly established occupations; but gradually, as one enquiry into industrial conditions after another showed that the same situation was to be found in every other occupation, the laws were extended to cover more and more industries until finally all factories and workshops came within their scope.

Yet right up to the present time, the climate of opinion in which the factory laws were first passed has given them a characteristic shape. As has been shown in an earlier chapter, it was part of the body of beliefs called *laissez faire* or Individualism that a man would not voluntarily submit to any contract of employment unless he believed it to be in his own interest and the gross unfairness in bargaining power between an employer, backed by his capital and superior knowledge, and an individual workman, faced by starvation as the only alternative to getting a job, was not realized. With such ideas it was natural to argue that any interference by the State in fixing hours of work or other terms of employment was an infringement of personal liberty that was altogether inadmissible in principle. Protective legislation for children could be accepted because one could not expect children to be able to bargain on equal terms with an employer; and when later, in 1844, women were brought under the factory laws, it could again be justified on the grounds that women were, in a sense, grown-up children who were unable to talk to employers as equals. But adult men were never brought within the scope of these laws and they still remain outside it.

As matters have turned out this has not worked to their disadvantage. In the many industries in which both men and women were employed—though on different jobs—it proved too difficult to have one set of conditions for women and another for the men, so the men got their protection, as was often said, 'behind the skirts of the women'; and in the predominantly male occupations, such as the metal industries and the mines, the growth of trade unionism soon enabled the men to demand better terms than the laws insisted on for women. As time went on there was no longer the same opposition to improved working conditions. Experience showed quite conclusively that long hours of work and unhealthy workplaces were definitely uneconomic, for overtired men and women, working in badly lit and unventilated places could not produce as well or as quickly as those with adequate leisure to recover from their fatigue; and the general standard of factory conditions came to be far in advance of the minimum laid down by law.

In looking back from the present day to the working conditions of the early nineteenth century that were so slowly—and apparently, so reluctantly—improved by factory and mines legislation, it is easy to jump to the conclusion that the employers in the new industries were exceptionally grasping, brutal and stony-hearted men. But this is looking at history backwards. The change from a predominantly rural to an increasingly urban life brought with it a great upheaval of settled ways of life and people who had been uprooted from habits which had been formed over many generations looked back with nostalgia on what had seemed to them a happier age. The heavy toil, insanitary conditions, overcrowded houses, the overwork of women and children and filthy conditions which had been taken for granted in the villages became a public scandal when people were gathered together in large towns far removed from the fields and fresh air. By putting it all into a new background it forced it on people's attention and by rousing the moral indignation of reformers it led to investigations which compelled the community to become aware of situations which had existed before but of which they had been ignorant or tolerant.

The gradual improvement of towns

The revelations made by these enquiries led many compassionate people to devote their lives to the protection of the most obviously unprotected groups in society but when many of these conditions of filth were shown to be a danger to all classes of the community the concern became much more widespread. The lack of water, sewers and fresh air which had been taken for granted in the villages became much more serious in the crowded towns where the death rate due to filth was so high that in such a large town as London, for example, the size of the population was only kept up by the constant

11. *Slum houses in 1899*

arrival of countrymen from the healthier rural areas. In the industrial towns where overcrowding was the rule—partly because housebuilding could not keep pace with the thousands coming into the factories, and partly because the rents that badly paid workers could afford to pay did not allow of anything more than the lowest type of shelter—the packing together of unwashed, underfed bodies led to epidemics which did not confine their ravages to the working people but spread to all classes. Cholera was a constant menace and during the worst of its visitations over 80,000 people died, 15,000 in London alone. Though the highest death-rates were in the poorest neighbourhoods, thousands of the richer people succumbed to this terrible disease.

In 1843 Edwin Chadwick, the Secretary to the Poor Law Commissioners, published his *Report on the Sanitary Conditions of the Labouring Population* which made the more comfortable groups in society realize the danger to themselves of living so close to these dirty crowded areas where were bred the diseases caused by lack of air, water and sanitation.

12. *An improvement: Peabody Square, Westminster. Model dwellings for the poor set up by a charitable American*

Chadwick insisted that not only physical health was at stake; but to compel people to live in dirty hovels with no means of keeping themselves or their houses even moderately clean, was a sure path to depravity and degradation, to crime as well as disease. The whole nation would suffer unless more attention was given to the provision of decent housing and the prevention of ill health caused by dirt. The first Public Health Act was passed in 1848 and, although it was a long time before great headway was made against ignorance, vested interests and the opposition of private owners (the first really effective Housing Act was not passed until 1890) the foundations of collective action were definitely laid.

Most of this 'environmental' legislation, i.e. laws to improve the general surroundings, was directed towards the control of sanitary conditions in order to maintain a minimum standard of cleanliness, not to the provision of houses. It was assumed that private enterprise would build whatever houses were needed for profit and it was not until well into the present century that local authorities began to play a significant part in house-building. But for many thousands of low paid workers the rents demanded by speculative builders were more than they could afford and many experiments were made by charitable bodies to try to get over this difficulty. Many Housing Associations were formed which proved that it was possible to build homes to be let at rents which workers could afford to pay and which would yet provide a modest return on the capital invested. The most famous of these was the Peabody Trust founded in 1862 by an American philanthropist who gave in all half a million pounds for the erection of blocks of flats (many of which still bear his name) for the housing of working class families of small income.

Educating the poor

Voluntary effort laid the foundation for Government action in education as well as in housing. Two bodies—the National Society and the British and Foreign Schools Society had been established early in the century to provide elementary education for the children of working class families. They were anxious that children should be able to read and write in order to read the Bible and thus gain some religious instruction. At first they depended entirely on voluntary contributions but after they had been in operation for some time the Government began to give them some small sums towards their costs. In the second half of the century there was widespread dismay over the illiteracy and ignorance of the mass of the population. Other countries—in particular, Germany and America—were beginning to be serious competitors to British industry and commerce and the idea was gaining ground that part, at least, of their success was owing to their better educational systems. The determining factor, however, was giving the vote to the working classes in the two acts of 1867 and 1888 for they were so much more numerous than those who already had the vote that many feared what might be the outcome of the political power wielded by the ignorant masses. Consequently, 'We must educate our masters' became the popular slogan. The first Education Act was passed in 1870 to provide for the setting up of schools in all areas, financed out of local rates and although the voluntary bodies continued to function and to receive grants from public funds, the local authorities from that time came to be the main providers of schools and employers of teachers.

(ii) The problem of poverty

Factory legislation, Public Health Acts and schools could begin to establish minimum standards in their respective fields but they could do nothing to help in the most serious of all problems with which an individual might have to cope—the loss of an income on which to live. In a community of wage-earners (and that is what the country was rapidly becoming) there are a number of circumstances which may prevent one from earning—old age, sickness, unemployment, accidents are the principal ones. It is with these disasters in life (for old-age was then a disaster) that the next phase in the development of society providing for its members is concerned. Each was the subject of much experiment and much controversy before a pattern began to emerge.

The workhouse

The Poor Law Amendment Act, 1834, had set itself the task of compelling people to strive for independence by making poor relief as unpleasant as possible and one of the ways in which it hoped to achieve this end was by insisting on the 'workhouse test', i.e. no able-bodied man could get any help from poor relief funds other than by agreeing to go into the workhouse. At the same time it recognized that there were some classes in the community whom no amount of deterrent treatment could make independent. People who were old and infirm could not provide for themselves, however sharp the goad; and from the beginning of the new regime, Boards of Guardians were permitted to give them relief at home. But it was *permission*, not compulsion, and the Central Authority deliberately refrained from giving any direction on the matter.

The practice varied from district to district. For example, at one period during the eighties, when the national proportion of those relieved in workhouses was 24% it was over 59% in the metropolitan boroughs. In some areas the offer of the 'House' was used as a lever to persuade relations who were not legally liable to offer money or a home to old people so as not to face the social stigma of having a member of the family in the workhouse; but often also it was intended as a kindness for when a Relieving Officer found an old man or woman living alone in an insanitary cottage with nobody to care for him he felt that he would be better looked after in the House. When 'out relief' was given it was almost invariably inadequate. Harassed, overworked officials had neither the time nor the skill to discover exactly what resources the applicant had at his disposal and they therefore tended to assume that these were always under-stated and that there was some little nest egg hidden away. Even so there was no doubt of the preference of applicants for out relief rather than the workhouse.

When there are hundreds of separate local bodies maintaining institutions it is impossible to make any fair generalizations about them. Some Guardians were generous and sympathetic; others were just the opposite. In some Houses the food was good and plentiful but even in these it was not the kind to which the inmates had been accustomed nor was it possible to take account of individual tastes. Even in the best run Houses a strict routine was thought to be essential to good economic administration and it was difficult for old people to adjust themselves to a schedule run by the clock after a lifetime of a different way of living. Perhaps the worst thing to bear was the lack of privacy and the isolation at one and the same time. Usually there was only one large common room in which all sat together during the day, with nothing to occupy them and nothing to talk about. They were rarely allowed to go out very much, and if friends were permitted to visit them they had to carry on their conversation under the

13. *The Women's Common Room, St James's Parish Workhouse, 1808. According to the standards of the time a good one and its inmates 'people of comparatively good character'*

eyes and within hearing of everybody else. Sometimes the presence in their midst of old people with unpleasant personal habits, caused untold misery to others who were forced to spend the long, weary days in their company.

At first sight it might seem that of all the possible vicissitudes of life, there is none for which people would be more likely to make their early provision than old age. Most of us are inclined to be optimistic about our fate—or perhaps we are unwilling to face realities—and we assume that illness or accidents or the loss of jobs are all more likely to affect other people rather than ourselves. But also, equally, most of us take it for granted that we will live to a ripe old age; we rarely believe that we are marked for an early grave. So could not the majority be expected to provide for old age even if they are too improvident to save for other purposes? This certainly was the view of the nineteenth-century reformers who were anxious to improve the conditions of the mass of the population. Yet, in fact, as soon as records began to be collected the opposite was found to be the case.

Before 1890 no distinction as to the ages of paupers was made in the official returns of those in receipt of Poor Law assistance; for although the Boards of Guardians were empowered to give out-relief to the non-able bodied there was no legal definition of the age at which a man might be presumed to have ceased to be able bodied. Some Boards fixed one age, some another and some varied according to circumstances. But in that year figures were got out for the first time estimating the number over the age of 60 years who were receiving poor relief on a certain day—August 1, 1890. The figures could not be accurate for the compulsory registration of births did not begin until 1845, so that anybody in the older age groups of 1890 would have to depend on parish registers, entries in family Bibles or memory for their knowledge, and, as it was known that the authorities were generally inclined to be more lenient in their treatment of the aged than that of any other group, there may have been some temptation towards overstatement. But there was, of course, a limit to this. The applicant must evidently have *looked* aged and infirm before there was any likelihood of his statement being accepted. Even allowing for some inaccuracies the picture that emerged from the figures was very startling, for it showed that the number relieved increased with each higher age group rising from 5·3% in the 60–65 group to 30% in the over 80's.

Poverty and old age

The House of Commons therefore ordered a return to be made of the ages of all paupers during a period of 12 months and this fully confirmed the returns made on August 1. It showed that whereas the degree of pauperism of the whole population was less than 5% it was 20% for the 65–70 group, about 30% for those between 70 and 75, and for those over 75 it was very nearly 40%. It must be remembered that at this time about one-third of the population were sufficiently well off to be unlikely ever to be in need of charity or public aid so that the proportions of the *working classes* receiving relief were much higher than these national figures. The conclusion to be drawn from these figures was that, contrary to the common opinion, the principal cause of pauperism was, in fact, nothing more nor less than old age.

From this time there began to be a strong movement amongst compassionate people to do something to lessen the misery of the old. Two schools of thought soon became apparent—one which believed that with adequate encouragement and organization, the majority of people could insure themselves for their future needs; the other which was convinced that most were prevented by circumstances from doing this and that the only practicable solution was for a pension to be provided from State funds.

The first group based their beliefs on the fact that a comparatively small sum paid as an insurance premium during the early years of a man's working life would, if left to increase by compound interest, provide a decent subsistence pension 50 years later. The wage earner differed from the business or professional man in that the latter can expect to enjoy a larger income as he is promoted to positions of greater responsibility. The worker, on the contrary, got his higher income when he was about 21, for his wage rate was the same as that of older men in the same occupation, but his work was likely to be more regular because of his health and fitness. The young bachelor did not generally think seriously of the future when his domestic obligations would be heavier, and was inclined to spend what he earned. Later, when he had a wife and family, there was no surplus out of which to save. Even the minority who tried to put something aside through the Friendly Societies had no security for, as has been shown, many of these societies were so badly managed and were based on such faulty calculations that they often became insolvent and their members lost the benefit for which they had made such great sacrifices.

Compulsory self-help?

A scheme was therefore proposed which would compel young workers between the ages of 18 and 21 to insure themselves in a fund which would be guaranteed by the State; and it was calculated that a total premium of £15 paid during these three years would be sufficient to provide a pension of 4*s*. a week from the age of 70 until death.

The scheme seemed attractive but there were many snags in it.

(1) It was asking an enormous amount of a young man just starting out in adult life to think half a century ahead and imagine himself in old age. The years of early manhood were about the only ones in a workman's span of life when he could afford to enjoy a few pleasures, because he had a little of his wages left after buying the bare essentials. After that short period the needs of his wife and children would take every penny he earned. Was it fair to expect him to give up even that fleeting time of being carefree?

(2) For the large number of young men serving an apprenticeship there was no possibility of saving such a large sum. Until the term of the apprenticeship was ended at the age of

21 their wages were so small as to require help from their families.

(3) The scheme also virtually excluded women from the provision offered for although probably all working class girls were employed for the few years before marriage their earnings were so low that no amount of self-sacrifice could enable them to save the amount needed. After marriage they withdrew from wage-earning entirely, for the typical Victorian family consisted of 5 to 7 children and by the time child-bearing and care came to an end the mother was too old to earn or save.

(4) The finance of the scheme depended on the long period for which the premium remained untouched; so even if all the above difficulties could be overcome nobody could benefit for another half-century. Meanwhile there were hundreds of thousands of old people in need.

It was this dilemma that caused the second scheme to gain adherents, but the idea of a pension provided out of public funds as a statutory right was so breathtakingly revolutionary that even those who were convinced that insurance was impracticable hesitated to accept it. Of the general desire to lessen the privations of those who had lived thrifty, industrious and self-respecting lives there was no doubt; the problem was how to do this without, at the same time, wasting the nation's money on those whose poverty was the result of their own dissolute and spendthrift characters. How could one distinguish the sheep from the goats?

One suggestion made was that the Government should encourage self-help by offering to double the premiums paid by a contributor to a Friendly Society as his membership was proof of his anxiety to provide for himself. But, as it was pointed out, it was a mean-spirited man who sacrificed his children's welfare in order to save for his own needs as an old man. For the majority of low paid workers wise thrift consisted in spending on food and clothing for himself and his family so as to preserve his own fitness for work and the health of the next generation, however difficult his declining years might thus become.

The idea of a State Pension

The only alternative to this deadlock, argued Charles Booth, was to offer a State pension of, say, 5*s*. a week to everybody who wished to claim it at the age of 65, irrespective of need or merit. Only in this way could the provision for old age be rid of the taint of pauperism.

The proposal was met by a storm of criticism. It was said that the cost would be prohibitive; that the incentive to thrift would be destroyed; that the sense of responsibility to the old members of the family would be lost; and that, worst of all, it would be a disastrous precedent and lead to other impoverished classes of the community, in addition to the old, looking to the State to get them out of their difficulties. And finally, it was argued, State help remains State help whatever the name it goes by. Pauperism is still pauperism whether the gift is called a pension or 'out-relief'.

14. *Police inspecting homeless vagrants, 1872. An etching (by Gustave Doré) from a life drawing*

To all these criticisms Charles Booth had an answer. Far from destroying thrift, a pension made the attempt to save worth while. Out-relief which was not given until a man was destitute penalized thrift. Those who had struggled throughout their working lives to put by what they could were unable to get any assistance until all their resources were exhausted, whilst those who had made no effort to save *had* to be relieved. If, however, a pension were to be given irrespective of savings it would give people hope, and encouragement to do whatever they could for themselves in the knowledge that the pension would be the solid foundation on which their own resources would rest. Further, out-relief, in any case, involved a detailed enquiry into the life and means of the applicant, and the loss of dignity and self respect involved made the sensitive person ready to starve rather than submit to it. A pension of 5*s*. a week would not be sufficient to maintain a person, but it would give that element of security which would make further effort worth while. Nor was the cost really too serious, for it was calculated that it would cost only £18,000,000 a year and at the same time would save £2,000,000 on Poor Law expenditure.

Yet the fear of undermining individual independence was so strong that, despite Booth's arguments, the Old Age Pensions Bill when it was introduced in 1908 did not provide pensions as a right for all: it proposed a pension of 5*s*. a week to those over 70 who had an income of less than £31 10*s*. 0*d*. a year. There were some die-hards who opposed it on principle as a direct blow to independence, but they were few; there were more who supported it reluctantly because it did not go far enough, but who were prepared to accept it as a first step towards a more radical reform. But how anxious the majority were to ensure that some action should be taken to lessen the misery of old age can be seen from the fact that the Bill passed its Third Reading by 315 votes to 10.

In the country the Act was welcomed as evidence of the newly recognized responsibility of the State to its members. As the weekly newspaper *Nation* said: 'The nation has made up its mind to a fuller responsibility for the condition of the poor, and it is not the aged poor alone who will benefit by the new spirit.'

When the Act had had time to become effective it was found that, of all the people in England and Wales over the age of 70, three-fifths were old age pensioners. The proportion varied from one place to another according to the social composition of the community, varying from 267 per thousand in Bournemouth to 778 in Bermondsey and 801 in Northamptonshire. Small as the pension was, the drop in the number of elderly paupers proved how right Booth had been in arguing that it would not prevent people from striving to keep their independence by their own savings, for the numbers on out-relief dropped from 168,096 in 1906 to 8,563 in 1913.

The outbreak of the First World War in 1914 brought new problems. The rise in the cost of living made it essential to increase the amount of the pension, but also the shortage of labour due to millions of men leaving industry and going into the armed forces made it necessary to persuade older people to come back into employment and this led to a slackening of the means test. At the end of the war the Chancellor of the Exchequer set up a Committee to consider what alterations in the system of Old Age Pensions should be introduced and it is interesting to see how radically ideas had changed in so short a time. The thought of State provision for the ups and downs of life no longer seemed novel or revolutionary; even those who had been most bitterly opposed now accepted it as necessary and had come to believe that the means test caused needless irritation and unhappiness as well as tending to penalize thrift and industry. Yet to provide a pension as a matter of right for everybody, whether rich or poor, seemed an unjustifiable extravagance. The question was 'How could one define the people to whom the pensions should be given without enquiry into their means, without at the same time giving it to the hundreds of thousands who were perfectly able to provide for themselves?' The solution to this dilemma was found in the development of the systems of compulsory national insurance for sickness and unemployment and it is to these that we now turn.

(iii) Social reform, 1906–1914

The period from 1906 to the beginning of the First World War was one of great activity in the field of social legislation. In fact, it would be true to say that most of the developments that we now think of as part of the Welfare State are built on the foundations laid during that exciting time. The opportunity was provided by the rise to power of the Liberal Party which was pledged to many reforms; but one must be careful not to lay too much stress on these party changes for the anxiety to improve the lot of the masses of the population was not confined to any one political group. Indeed it is worth remembering that Charles Booth, who did more than anybody else to open people's eyes to the extent and causes of poverty and who fought so hard for a State Old Age Pension free of a means test, was a Conservative. Yet on the whole it is true that at the time of which I am now speaking the Liberal Party showed a much greater readiness than the Conservatives to bring in the help of the State in the protection of the weaker sections of society, and their success in the election of 1906 enabled them to begin a great series of legislative experiments.

It is doubtful, however, if they would have done so much had it not been for the influence of the new Labour Party. During the last decades of the nineteenth century there had been many progressive thinkers, both inside and outside the trade union movement, who had tried to persuade the unions of the need for a separate political party. Efforts had already been made to get working men elected to Parliament so that they could act as spokesmen on labour matters with first-hand knowledge and experience; but the majority of trade unionists were quite content that these 'Lib-Labs' as they came to be called should remain within the Liberal fold. They remained unmoved by the arguments of the minority that there was something absurd and inconsistent in the hard fought negotiations which they carried on with their employers to get better working conditions and wages when, immediately after, they went to the polls to elect these same men to Parliament as their political representatives. The thing which did more than anything else to change their attitude was the famous House of Lords ruling in the Taff Vale dispute, when the employers brought an action against one of the railway unions for losses incurred as a result of the actions of the union members. In that dispute, the decision was given that, contrary to the established belief of a quarter of a century, damages could be demanded from a trade union for the acts of their members during a trade dispute and the unions, faced with bankruptcy if many such claims were made against them, became convinced that an independent political organization was essential to their safety. But nobody was prepared for the rapid growth of the new party and its astonishing success in getting 29 members elected to the new Parliament. It was obvious that a new force, and one that had to be reckoned with, had burst into the political arena.

The new party was not socialist and that is why the name 'Labour' was chosen. (In fact, it was not until after the end of the First World War that its programme became distinctively socialist rather than liberal or radical). But it came with a new determination to get things done to improve the conditions of the working population. Its members acted as a kind of ginger group constantly spurring the Liberal Government to introduce the reforms that had been discussed for so long.

The Royal Commission on the Poor Laws

Interest in the 'social question' was further stimulated by the results of the investigations of the Royal Commission on the Poor Laws and the Relief of Distress which had been appointed in 1905. The detailed reports it issued during the next few years threw a flood of light over the whole field of poverty. Its two final reports published in 1909, the Majority Report signed by 14 Commissioners and the Minority Report signed by 4 who did not agree with the others, brought sharply into the forefront of political controversy the contrasted views of the opposing schools of thought.

The Majority Report represented what might be called the orthodox 'Individualist' opinion at the stage it had reached in the early twentieth century. It recognized, as would not have been done 30 or 40 years earlier, that the individual is not always master of his fate and that he cannot maintain his independence unless the social organization is suitable; and the need for him to be protected by the community in many circumstances was fully accepted. But those who held this view were always afraid that further State action might undermine self-reliance and teach men to look to others rather than to rely on themselves as a normal thing, instead of as a last resort.

The Minority Commissioners started from an entirely different standpoint. They believed that a great deal of poverty was due to the failure of the community rather than of the

15. *A photograph, in old age, of Sidney and Beatrice Webb, who were mainly responsible for the Minority Report of the Royal Commission on the Poor Laws and for many of the ideas on which the Welfare State is based.*

individual and that policy must be directed towards discovering and removing the causes of poverty, not simply to relieving the misery of the destitute. If you could change living conditions so as to prevent ill-health and build up a medical service to deal with sickness before it became serious, for example, or if you could so reorganize industry that irregular employment was reduced, you would enable a man to remain the independent breadwinner of the family, instead of simply considering how you could get him and his family fed when he was unable to earn a wage. The fact that the Minority Commissioners were exceptionally able and well-informed people (one of them was Mrs Sidney Webb who with her husband was one of the most outstanding and effective reformers of the time) did an enormous amount to get their views widely discussed and largely accepted.

During the few years after the Liberal Government came into power, therefore, there was a burst of law-making somewhat similar to the one recently experienced during 1945–50 when the Labour Government came into power after the Second World War. In addition to the Old Age Pensions Act already discussed, the Trade Boards Act established the first machinery for the abolition of 'sweating' in those occupations in which ignorant and exploited wage-earners had been unable to build up trade unions to protect themselves; a network of Labour Exchanges was set up all over the country to make it easier for men to discover where jobs were available, compensation for industrial accidents was extended, a School Medical Service and School Meals were provided to look after the health of the children; and most important of all the National Insurance Act introduced what has now come to be the normal method employed in the effort to preserve the minimum standard of living of the workers' family during the usual troubles of life.

For an industrialized community which is entirely dependent on wages as the sole source of the standard of living, anything which interrupts regular earning can bring disaster to a family and the two most common causes of this are sickness and inability to find a job.

The sick

Medical care for sick people was provided in a number of ways. Originally the workhouses had made little distinction between the sick and the rest of their inmates; but in 1865 the death of two paupers in circumstances which seemed to point to serious neglect led to official enquiry and revealed a very disquieting state of affairs. Wards were insanitary and overcrowded, food inadequate and badly cooked and all the nursing was left to fellow paupers. Public indignation at this hard-heartedness towards suffering was mingled with alarm at the possible spread of infectious diseases, and sweeping changes were introduced. Separate Poor Law institutions exclusively for the sick were set up with resident doctors, paid nurses and equipment similar to that found in ordinary hospitals. So great was the improvement that many people who would not have dreamed of applying for Poor Relief in the usual way came to look upon these infirmaries as general State hospitals entirely dissociated from the Poor Law.

There were also many voluntary hospitals which had been founded by charitable endowments throughout the centuries and these had increased in number and size during the nineteenth century. But these had not necessarily been built in the most densely populated areas, since they had been established in the neighbourhood that the charitable founder happened to know and most of the new industrial towns were sadly lacking in provision. The overcrowding was so great, particularly in the out-patients department that it was often said that the hospitals created as much disease as they cured for the waiting rooms were so filled with men, women and children suffering from a diversity of diseases that they were themselves a cause of infection; and harrassed doctors could do little more than hand out bottles of medicine after a cursory examination.

In many of the larger towns there were medical missions and free dispensaries run by various religious bodies which offered free doctoring, and sometimes special foods, in return for attendance at religious services, but neither hospitals nor dispensaries could provide the income to replace the lost earnings of the sick man they were trying to cure. The Boards of Guardians were empowered to give out-relief to those who were destitute and they had the duty of providing medical attention for those in receipt of it. But the doctors they appointed were so overworked and underpaid that it was difficult for them to give the care required. No provision was made for nursing or for medicines unless the doctor gave these out of his own pocket—as, in fact, very many of them did—so not only was the death rate high but those who survived took much longer to get over their illness than they would have done with proper care.

Immense efforts were made by the workers themselves to build up organizations to deal with the problem, but these were much more concerned with trying to provide a substitute income during the time a man was off work through sickness than with medical attention. Hundreds of thousands subscribed to the Friendly Societies for this purpose but we know that these often failed and left their members without resources despite the sacrifices they had made to save. Even if the society kept its head above water members dropped out because of low wages or periods of unemployment when they fell into arrears. It was calculated that every year there was an average of 25,000 lapsed policies and it was fairly clear that the majority of workers could not make adequate provision without some assistance.

Many of the trade unions, particularly the big craft unions, also had schemes of voluntary insurance through which a sick member became entitled to a weekly benefit for a period of time if he had a medical certificate to show that he was unable to carry on his work. In most cases the worker was expected to make his own arrangements with the doctor but in others, notably in the mining areas, the union entered into a contract with a local doctor to attend its sick members.

A landmark: The National Insurance Act of 1911

Mr Lloyd George who was then Chancellor of the Exchequer had been very much impressed by what he had learned of a scheme operating in Germany for compulsory sickness insurance and he believed that a similar scheme could be introduced into this country. He was convinced that the enormous number of subscribers to the Friendly Societies and the voluntary insurance funds of the unions were evidence of the desperate anxiety of working men to provide for periods of sickness, but he argued that it was unfair that they should be expected to bear all the burden themselves. It was so important to keep up a healthy labour force, both for employers and for the whole community, that they should be prepared to contribute to the cost and he proposed a system of compulsory national insurance to be financed by the weekly premiums of employers and employed, and by an additional subvention from public funds. By the National Insurance Act, 1911, therefore, we established the three-sided system of compulsory insurance which has become the pattern for social security funds not only in this country but in a great part of the world.

From the administrative point of view the Act made a bold experiment, for, instead of setting up entirely new machinery for the purpose, it built upon the foundations already laid by the workers themselves in their Friendly Societies and trade

16. *Lloyd George in 1911*

unions. Any such body could apply to become an Approved Society to administer the Act, provided it was not conducted for profit and that its constitution left its affairs in the absolute control of the members. It was bound to provide the benefits set down in the Act, but if its periodic valuation showed any surplus it could use this as it liked in additional benefits. These might take the form of an increase in the cash weekly allowance or payment towards the cost of treatments—dental, convalescent homes and the like—not set down in the Act.

The benefits provided by law were:

(1) Sickness benefit, i.e. a weekly payment of 7*s.* a week for men (less for women) for a period of 26 weeks. The cash benefits changed later as money values altered after the war.

(2) Disablement benefit, i.e. a continuation of the weekly cash benefit at a reduced rate when (1) had been exhausted.

(3) Maternity benefit, i.e. a lump sum paid on the confinement of an insured woman or of the wife of an insured man.

(4) Medical benefit, i.e. medical treatment, including prescribed medical and surgical appliances and medicines.

The scheme covered every manual worker (with the exception of those in the service of the Crown who got these benefits as part of their conditions of service) and all non-manual workers earning less than £160 a year, i.e. those in clerical and distributive trades or similar occupations where the economic circumstances were similar to those of the average manual wage-earner.

The Approved Societies varied greatly in size and efficiency. The large well-run ones with an assured income drawn from the weekly contributions of members and their employers, with the added help from the Exchequer, were soon able to offer considerable benefits in addition to those laid down by law, whilst small or badly run societies could only just comply with their legal requirements.

The new scheme, covering as it did practically the whole working population, offered a way out of the dilemma posed by the Old Age Pensions. The difficulty there had been to find a way to provide an income as a statutory right for the older citizens that did not penalize thrift without at the same time giving public funds to richer people who had no need of extra help. The insurance system provided an excellent dividing line. The weekly wage-earners, whether manual or non-manual, consisted of just those income groups for which the community was anxious to make a dignified, secure provision outside the Poor Law, and an Act passed in 1926, a Contributory Old Age Pensions Act, achieved this end. Everybody in the Health Insurance scheme was automatically included. For the first five years after reaching pensionable age (65 for men and 60 for women) he or she became entitled to a pension from the funds of the Approved Society to which he belonged and after those five years, also automatically, became entitled to the same pension from the Exchequer. There was thus no need for any enquiry into his own resources and so it was well worth his while to try to save as much as he could whilst he was earning in the knowledge that the pension would be added to what he had himself. The only group still dependent on a means test were those who, for one reason or another, were not included in the wide boundaries of the Health Insurance scheme.

The unemployed

It was much more difficult to work out a scheme for unemployment insurance than for sickness. Very few people want to be ill and even those who are inclined to magnify any slight sickness can generally be spotted by a competent doctor. But it is nothing like so easy to discover whether a man is out of work because there is less demand for the kind of job he is able to do, or because he is not very active in looking for work, or because he is unwilling to try and learn something new when his own occupation is declining. The few unions which had organized voluntary unemployment insurance for their members had had to find ways of protecting their funds from the work-shy and the fact that they were composed entirely of highly skilled men made it possible for them to do this. They did it in two ways: (1) by strictly limiting the number of weeks for which benefit was paid and (2) by setting up bureaux to act as clearing houses between employers and workers. They persuaded firms to notify them of vacancies and most were quite ready to do this for it saved them a lot of bother in getting hold of skilled labour quickly. The union could then test whether a claimant was involuntarily unemployed (and it was, of course, only involuntary unemployment they were trying to deal with) by offering the man the vacancy that had been notified and stopping benefit if he refused a job for which he was suitable.

At that time, however, there were no general Employment Exchanges (and the men covered by these union schemes were only a little over half a million at the beginning of this century). An unemployed man had to tramp the neighbourhood—or even sometimes the whole country—looking for a factory notice which said 'Hands wanted'. Apart from this, all he could depend on was hearsay or the help of a friend who might tell him that such and such a firm was taking on more labour. Before any general provision for the unemployed could be introduced, therefore, it was essential to set up a network of offices to which employers could notify their demands for workers and to which workers could apply for jobs. By the Labour Exchanges Act, 1909, such a system was brought into being but, excellent as was the idea, it took a long time to get into good working order. Workers are not interchangeable units. There are hundreds and hundreds of different kinds of work and the man who can do one job cannot do the others; so before a Labour Exchange officer can tell if it is sensible to tell an applicant of a particular vacancy he must know a great deal about the various processes in the industries in his locality. No information of this kind was available in 1909. Nowadays, after more than half a century of experience, a very detailed classification of jobs has been built up and is continually revised to take in new techniques; but when the exchanges were first set up the officers had simply to guess, and often they sent completely unsuitable men to the jobs that had been notified. This led to unwillingness on both sides to use the exchanges and it took a long time to get over this bad start.

It was realized that it would be impossible to have an efficient scheme of unemployment insurance until there were proper means of testing whether a man was really involuntarily unemployed or not, so the Government decided to begin with an experiment on a comparatively small scale. Part I of the National Insurance Act which established the health insurance scheme covered the vast majority of working people but Part II which set up the unemployment scheme applied only to one group of occupations—building, construction work, shipbuilding and engineering—which between them employed 2¼ million workpeople. The finance of the scheme was the same as for the health insurance, i.e. compulsory weekly contributions by employers and workers paid by means of putting stamps on a card, with an additional subvention from State funds. In order to claim benefit an unemployed person had to register at a Labour Exchange (the name was changed to Employment Exchange in 1917) and be prepared to apply for any job suitable to his skill and previous experience. If he refused a job that was considered suitable

17. *A Labour Exchange, photographed in February, 1910*

(and provision was made for an appeal to a Tribunal if there was a difference of opinion), he could not draw benefit and, in any case, the number of weeks for which he could draw the allowance was limited in proportion to the number of weeks for which he had paid contributions.

(iv) Mass unemployment in the great depression

The belief expressed at the time that the operation of these rules would remove the greater part of unemployment was justified by the experience gained during the first year's operation; for the amount of unemployment which continued after the right to benefit had been exhausted was only 1% of the total in the insured occupations. Whether this would have continued it is impossible to say for the First World War broke out in 1914 and completely changed the whole situation. During the war there was practically no unemployment at all, for people were needed for the armed forces, making of munitions and the maintenance of civilian life; so there was no opportunity of discovering how far the scheme would stand up to all the problems it was designed to help solve. And as soon as the war was over there was such widespread fear of the dislocation that would accompany the transition from a war to a peace economy that the scheme was extended in 1920 to cover almost the whole working population.

The scheme as planned never had a chance to get into its stride for at the same time as the passing of the Act there began the most prolonged and serious period of unemployment that this country has ever known. From 1920 until the outbreak of the Second World War in 1939 there were only one or two very short periods when the percentage of unemployed fell below 10% and there were several years when it was over 22%. Even that does not tell the whole story for the unemployment was not spread evenly over the country. For example, in a year when the average rate of unemployment was 12%, the rate was nearly 30% amongst iron and steel workers, 27% in the shipbuilding industry and 24% in iron-founding; and when the national rate rose to 23% during the worst years of the depression, there were between a third and a half of all men out of work in the textile, mining and shipbuilding areas. Thus from its commencement the scheme had to try to cope with types and amounts of unemployment for which it had not been designed, because we had never known them before. For the next twenty years the country was compelled to try one thing after another in the attempt to deal with the poverty and misery brought by this chronic mass unemployment and it was largely due to this that, by the time the Second World War started, we had come to have entirely different ideas of what we expected from a system of compulsory national insurance from those on which the scheme had originally been based.

The insurance schemes were not intended to guarantee a minimum subsistence income to a family; their objective was very much more limited. Nobody was so foolish as to think that 7*s*. a week was enough to maintain a household, even taking into account the much lower standards of living of the mass of the population and the difference in the value of money. The insurance benefit was designed to be a solid foundation for self-help, to make it worth while for a man to strive to save for his future needs in the knowledge that his savings would be an *addition* to the weekly benefit and not a substitute for it, as was the case with Poor Relief based on a means test. There seemed a good deal of evidence to show that if a wage-earner was sure of even this modest sum for a limited period he could keep his nose above water. As the condition for claiming benefit was that the man was unable to find a job it was, in a sense, a replacement of wages, and as wages were not determined by the size of his family, but by the work he was doing, it took no account of his family responsibilities. Moreover, the scheme was insurance—not relief—and that meant that everybody who paid the same premium had the same right to benefit, irrespective of his individual circumstances.

Long-term unemployment

Nobody could have foreseen the extent and nature of the unemployment that struck the country between the two wars.

Ups and downs in employment had already begun to be recognized. There were the long-term cycles of prosperity and depression (see Chapter 2) and there were the seasonal variations which occurred in a great many industries. Both these caused interruptions in the amount of labour demanded and the worker who was thrown out of employment needed resources to keep him going until the demand in his occupation revived. What nobody could have known was the profound change in the whole structure of industry that now took place. The big industries on which England's economic prosperity had been based—coal-mining, textiles, shipbuilding—declined rapidly, partly because of the rapid growth of industrialization in other parts of the world, and partly because of the rise of new industries which competed with them—oil instead of coal, for example, and rayon in place of cotton. As a result, the numbers of workers needed by the old industries fell quickly and drastically; however long their old employees waited to be taken on again, there was little chance

18. *The Great Depression, an unemployed man photographed in Wigan in 1939*

of ever being employed again in the same kind of work. Thousands of people, therefore, were out of work, not for a couple of weeks or so, but for months and years at a time. This was something of which we had had no experience and it was a type of unemployment for which the insurance scheme was not designed and which it was not capable of dealing with. There were four big differences:

(1) A small secure sum supplemented by one's own savings can keep a family going for a short time. One can cut down expenditure to the bare essentials. But the longer the period lasts the more change there is in what are 'bare essentials'. Not only do savings become exhausted but it becomes impossible to put off any longer the purchases of many things. New boots *must* be bought for the children; clothes wear out and must be replaced, etc.

(2) The right to benefit was limited to so many weeks in a year and no further benefit could be claimed until more contributions had been paid. But those out of work for years could not pay any premiums as they were not working and thus could only turn to the Poor Law.

(3) Maintenance for a few weeks is constructive if there is a good chance of being taken into the job again; but maintenance alone does not solve the problem if the employment has gone for good.

(4) The longer the unemployment lasts the more important it is to take into account the number of people in the household. If the loss of earnings lasts only two or three weeks, you can argue that insurance benefit which is a substitute for wages is no more concerned with the size of the family than are wages; but the larger the family the more quickly are savings exhausted and you cannot continue to argue this way when the children are starving.

Looking back on the situation 30 or 40 years later we can see that the mass unemployment was caused by unprecedented changes in the structure of industry and the direction of trade, but people living at the time could not understand this, for it was right outside their experience. They thought of it as a 'worse than usual' depression, exaggerated by the war and confidently believed that if only they could weather the next few months everything would go on as before. They recognized that the sufferings of the unemployed were not due to their own misdeeds or lack of foresight and there were strong views expressed that it would be unfair to force them to apply for poor relief with all the misery and loss of social standing involved. There was an additional reason for providing for them otherwise than by poor relief. The most heavily hit industries were not spread all over the country but were concentrated in certain localities and, as poor rates were a local tax, the worse off an area was by reason of the decline of its major industries, the heavier the tax it had to pay to maintain those who were destitute because of long term unemployment.

The acceptance of new ideas

During these years, therefore, there were introduced a whole series of temporary measures—temporary because it was always hoped that the next few months would see the turn of the tide. Men were allowed to claim insurance benefit after their rights had expired—sometimes for a stated period, sometimes at the discretion of the administering authorities; sometimes the extra benefit was confined to family men, sometimes extended to others. And each time the 'temporary' period came to an end the situation was found to be just as serious as before and a new measure had to be agreed. But there were two changes that were much more important than all others because of their influence on people's minds and their expectations of what could and should be done by an insurance system.

(1) A foundation for voluntary savings is quite useless when the period of unemployment is so long that it is out of the question for anybody to have any savings left; so the amount of benefit had to be raised to provide enough to exist on.

(2) Even more important was the recognition that a man with dependants needs more money for basic living than a single man and therefore, in 1922 Dependants Allowances were introduced. This cut so completely across the whole

idea of insurance (where benefits are related to premiums paid and have no relation either to resources or needs) that it, too, was thought of as a temporary expedient and it was assumed that as soon as things returned to 'normal' it would be given up. But mass unemployment went on and on and by the end of the nineteen-thirties Dependants Allowances had become so accepted a part of unemployment insurance and their social advantages were so widely recognized that it was realized that they should never be abandoned. This desperate measure to cope with a desperate situation had so changed public opinion that it came to be seen as an essential part of any future system of social security.

(v) Workmen's compensation

Even before the gradual change of opinion about the responsibility for misfortune, there had been one class of those in distress for whose relief a deterrent or punishing form of public assistance was obviously unjust—those injured in the course of their employment. According to Common Law an employer could be held liable for injuries to his workmen that were caused either by personal negligence or by lack of proper care in the choice of machinery or methods. This was sufficient when industry was on a small scale and it could be supposed that the employer was in touch with all that went on in his business; but with the increase of large-scale production the employer was represented by managers and foremen and it was difficult to fasten personal responsibility on to him; nor was he considered responsible for actions done by his agents in the firm. The Courts upheld what was known as the Doctrine of Common Employment, i.e. that a worker knowingly undertook the risk of accidents caused by his fellow employees and therefore could not sue the employer for any injury which resulted. This was, of course, nonsense, for workers had no alternative; it caused much bitter feeling, and much agitation for this doctrine to be given up. But even had the Doctrine of Common Employment been abolished, there would still have been difficulties, for figures were collected which showed that about half the accidents which took place in industry were not due to anybody's negligence. They were called Acts of God, i.e. pure accidents which were not due to carelessness or lack of foresight; for example, a burst boiler or a fall of rock in a mine. Whatever the cause of the accident the injured man and his family needed help and though it might be unjust to put the burden for these on the shoulders of the employer, this seemed the only practicable expedient. The supporters of this view argued that the employer would count this cost in the price of the goods he sold so that, in fact, it would be the purchasers who would eventually pay the cost of accidents occurring during their production and this was eminently fair.

A change in the law was achieved by the Workmen's (Compensation for Accidents) Act, 1897, which was based on the principle of compensation for accidents, not of the degree of the employer's liability. This introduced a new principle into English law—that financial responsibility exists even though there has been no break of contract and no wrong has been done by the employer or anybody acting on his behalf. It would probably have met with greater opposition had it not been confined to particularly dangerous trades. But once this new idea was accepted matters could not be allowed to rest there. The number of accidents in a comparatively safe trade is smaller than in a dangerous one, yet when an accident does occur the effect on the victim and his family is exactly the same as if the trade had been dangerous; and in 1906 the Act was extended to cover all accidents at work as well as specified industrial diseases. But there were even greater problems:

(1) The Act gave a legal claim to compensation but there was no guarantee that the injured man would get anything. This depended on his employer's solvency and, though most of the large firms insured against this liability, many smaller ones did not and went into liquidation when a big claim was made against them.

(2) It was difficult to prove that an injury and, even more, an occupational disease was sustained 'in the course of employment'. For example, if a man was knocked down by a

bus on his way to work and would not have been in that road had he not been going to work, was that in the course of his employment?

(3) As compensation was payment for loss of earnings it was calculated on the basis of previous earnings. But to give a lump sum to the widow and young family of a man killed at work did not provide for their upkeep as he would have done had he lived.

Dissatisfaction with the law grew continually stronger and the opinion began to develop that the most important thing to ensure was that the children of an injured worker should have the chance of growing up as healthy adults, and that this was more important than calculation of what his earnings had been. It is interesting to see the change of ideas from regarding compensation as payment for loss of income, to thinking of it as the means whereby the family's standard of living might be maintained.

The Act which was passed in 1923 did not introduce all these changes. Compensation was extended to all accidents and a number of specified diseases, incurred in the course of employment, but firms were not compelled to insure against their liability and many injured workers continued to lose the payments that were their legal due. And though the sum paid after a fatal accident took into account the time that children would remain dependent, compensation for a non-fatal accident was still based on previous earnings.

When the insurance system for sickness and disability developed there was a further complication, for sickness or disability due to employment was compensated by a different amount of money (and from a different source) from sickness or disability in ordinary life.

(vi) Faults in the social services

By the end of the thirties then, there was already a whole body of legislation whose object was to lift people out of poverty and help them to provide for the chief ups and downs of life. But, because of the way in which they had grown up, they were very haphazard. If you had known nothing of their history it would have been impossible for you to understand why they took that particular form. They were a hotch potch of different ideas, different methods of administration, and different amounts of benefit.

Differences are not necessarily a bad thing and uniformity is not always wise or sensible, provided there is a reason for the differences and they exist because they are the best way of meeting various purposes. But this was not the case with our social services.

(1) Take, for example, the most serious problem of all—the lack of income due to inability to earn through sickness or unemployment. If you were sick you claimed your benefit from the Approved Society of which you were a member and the amount you received depended on how efficiently and economically the Society was run. A small struggling society or one that was badly administered paid you the exact amount required by law; another could afford a whole list of extras—higher weekly amounts, or special treatments, or a period in a convalescent home. Yet although people got such different returns everybody paid the same weekly contribution. Moreover, however successful the society might be, the benefits were for the member alone; they took no account of the size of the family he had to support during his illness.

If, on the other hand, you were unemployed, you claimed your benefit from the Employment Exchange and you received the amount laid down by law; but you received an extra amount for your wife and dependent children.

Your sickness benefit was paid for a limited number of weeks after which you could claim a disability benefit at a much lower rate. Your unemployment benefit was also limited in duration by law, but in practice it was continually extended on account of the chronic nature of the mass unemployment between the two wars.

(2) If you were an 'insured contributor', i.e. you were within the scope of the Health and Unemployment Insurance Acts, you could claim an Old Age Pension at the age of 65 (for a man) and 60 (for a woman) for 5 years from the funds

of your Approved Society and after that you automatically qualified for a similar pension from State funds for the rest of your life, irrespective of your own resources. But if you were not an 'insured contributor' you could not get an Old Age Pension at any age unless you could show that your income was below a certain amount.

(3) All the benefits were too low to support life. Originally they had never been intended to do so, for they had been designed to give a solid foundation on which people could build their own provision from their own savings. But when hundreds of thousands of people were out of work for months or years at a time it was realized that no savings could possibly be sufficient to meet such need and that anything less than a basic minimum standard was useless. Gradually the unemployment benefits crept near to this minimum, but the sickness benefit did not.

(4) The benefits for women were lower than those for men. This was quite deliberate, for when the schemes began they were intended to be actuarially sound, i.e. the contributions received were supposed to equal the payments made. Women earn less than men and therefore it was right that they should pay smaller weekly contributions and so get smaller weekly benefits. But when it began to be accepted that the benefit must be enough to provide a minimum standard of living which took account of the size of the family, irrespective of the fact that the same contributions were paid by family men as by single men, this distinction could no longer be justified, for it costs as much to house, feed and clothe a woman as a man.

(5) If your loss of income was due to an accident, the position was even more complicated, for the Workmen's Compensation system was not a social service at all. It had originally been a legal claim against your employer for injuries for which he could be held responsible and had been extended to cover other accidents incurred in his service, simply because there seemed no other way of providing for them. If the employer had insured himself against this liability you would get compensation once you had legally

established your claim. But there was no compulsion on him to do so and you might fully make good your claim and then find he was bankrupt and could not pay you. It was also often very difficult to prove that the injury was sustained 'in the course of employment' and this was particularly so with certain diseases which could be contracted by anybody even though they might be more likely to occur in certain occupations. Thus there were always a great many law cases over these claims and this was not only expensive but also greatly reduced the security that the system was intended to give.

(6) The Unemployment Insurance scheme had been compelled by the force of circumstance to recognize that it costs more to keep a family than a childless couple and Dependants Allowances had been introduced and had become a necessary part of the payments made. Experience showed that an unskilled labourer with a large family might receive a larger amount when out of work than when he was employed because wages, of course, do not vary with the size of the family. This concentrated attention on a new problem which had before been ignored. All the social services described in this chapter were concerned with the difficulties that arise when earnings cease for one reason or another. It was assumed that a man who was able to work could maintain his family even if at a modest level. But now it had to be recognized that there might be severe poverty even when the father of the family was fully employed!

The great social investigators

It was due primarily to the efforts of three great social investigators that more attention was now paid to this problem. The first, Mr Seebohm Rowntree, who had made the important enquiries into the cause of poverty in York (see Chapter 2) showed that the majority of people—even those in the lower wage groups—were not in poverty all the time. There was a regular cycle through which most families passed. Most men earned enough to support themselves while they were single and when they were first married; but with each child that was born the difficulty of making ends meet grew greater and greater. When all the children were born (and remember that families, and particularly those of unskilled workers, were then fairly large) the burden was so great that many families were in real need. As the older children grew up and went into employment the burden became lighter until by the time all were working the family emerged from the shadow of dire poverty and was once again able to maintain a decent standard.

The second, Mr Colin Clark, in a very careful analysis of the distribution of income in the thirties, came to the conclusion that more than half the dependent children in the community at any one time were living in families whose income, per head, brought them perilously close to the poverty line. These families would not be in poverty when the heaviest burden of maintaining the children was over, but the undernourishment, bad housing and narrow experience of these children while they were growing up would have a lasting effect on their health and ability. No amount of good food, etc., later on could compensate for extreme poverty during childhood.

The third, Miss Eleanor Rathbone, in a book *The Disinherited Family* urged that the only way to prevent these bad effects was for the State to accept its responsibility for the welfare of its future citizens and help to support children when a man was in work, just as it had agreed to do when he was unemployed. Thus began the campaign for family allowances as one part of society's way of providing for minimum standards of living.

4. WHAT THE WELFARE STATE IS AND WHAT IT HAS DONE

The outbreak of the Second World War in 1939 triggered off the movement to get rid of all the faults in the social services mentioned in the last chapter. It may be that the memory of the miseries that had followed the First World War were still fresh in men's minds, or it may be that the tremendous national effort demanded by the Second heightened the sense of community; but no time was lost in setting to work to consider what could be done to ensure a happier way of life for the population when the war should be over. The first step was taken as early as 1941 when a committee was set up under the chairmanship of Sir William (later Lord) Beveridge called an 'Interdepartmental Committee on Social Insurance and the Allied Services to undertake with special reference to the inter-relation of the schemes, a survey of the existing national schemes of social insurance'. Originally the Chairman was the only member of the Committee who was not a senior civil servant, for it was supposed to concern itself mainly with problems of administration; but early in its deliberations Beveridge, with his wide knowledge and experience in this field, determined that a much more fundamental discussion was needed of the principles underlying social provision in general and he proposed to make this the main subject of the enquiry. In these circumstances the civil servants could no longer be members of the Committee; they continued to serve on it but only as consultants and the Chairman was solely responsible for the final recommendations. The famous Beveridge Report was published in 1942 and became the basis of the social policy of the subsequent period. It profoundly changed the whole concept of social legislation.

19. *The children at Snowsfield Primary School, London, in 1894 and in 1959*

The ideas behind the Beveridge Report

Beveridge started from the point that it was the duty of a civilized community to ensure that all its citizens had a minimum income to live on, a minimum of health, education and housing and that all social policy should be designed with this as its objective. This involved (*a*) an adequate income which took account of the number in the family, whether the individual was in work or unemployed or sick or old or injured, (*b*) facilities for education which were geared to the ability of the individual and not to the income of his parents, (*c*) a health service designed to prevent illness as far as possible, as well as to treat those who were sick, and (*d*) adequate housing at a price which people could afford to pay.

Most of these principles were accepted by all political parties, though there were differences of emphasis and differences of opinion about the methods by which the ends should be achieved. The Labour Party broadly agreed with Beveridge's main proposals and its overwhelming majority in the election of 1945 enabled it to introduce and carry through a packed programme of new legislation. In the five years of that Parliament a radical transformation of the social services took place.

Let us take each of Beveridge's chief objectives in turn.

(i) Basic security

Four acts were passed to try and ensure the maintenance of a basic income sufficient for subsistence in different circumstances: the National Insurance Act, 1946, the Industrial Injuries Act, 1946, the Family Allowances Act, 1945, and the National Assistance Act, 1948.

The existing insurance schemes had been planned primarily to offer some security to those sections of the population that had been found to run the most risk and to have least resources of their own to deal with it. They were intended to ensure just that small, but solid, foundation for private savings that would enable the majority of wage-earners to face periods of non-earning, whatever the cause, without being forced to apply for Poor Relief. And as the insurance benefit was designed to act, as it were, as a substitute for earnings, it took no more account of family responsibilities than wages did.

The new concept, introduced by Beveridge, was that insurance should be a provision *by* the whole community *for* the whole community. It should provide a safe scaffolding within which people could build their lives, whatever their income or social group. Instead of embodying the idea that the State should look after the 'underprivileged' or 'the poor', it was founded on the principle that an industrial economy, with its inevitable risks, might cause anybody, whatever his occupation or social grade, to suffer from the difficulties due to illness or old age or widowhood and so on; and therefore the whole community should accept a 'corporate' responsibility by including everybody within the schemes designed to cope with these risks. The new schemes differ, therefore, in many respects from the old.

Comprehensive social insurance

(1) National Insurance is no longer confined to particular classes or income ranges. It covers everybody over school-leaving age who has not yet reached the age of retirement for a pension. Contributors are divided into three classes:

(*a*) employed persons no matter what their work or what the pay received. This covers the highly paid company director just as much as the unskilled labourer and includes nearly 23 million people.

(*b*) self-employed persons, i.e. those in business on their own account who are working for gain but are not under the control of an employer—about 1½ million people.

(*c*) non-employed persons, i.e. all the rest, about a quarter of a million.

There are only two exceptions. The first is married women engaged only in housekeeping because they are covered by their husbands' insurance. Married women who are employed can choose whether to contribute or not; if they do, they receive benefits as individuals instead of as their husbands' dependants. The other exceptions are the self-employed or non-employed persons whose income is less than £208 a year.

(2) Instead of a number of separate schemes there is only one contribution which covers a large number of risks—sickness, unemployment, old age, widowhood, death, maternity.

(3) Unlike the earlier schemes the aim of the benefit is to be sufficient to provide a basic living. Whether the benefit does, in fact, provide a basic subsistence is always a matter of controversy. Since the Act was passed there has never been a period of stable prices and although both contributions and benefits have been raised many times since 1946 there are often times when prices race ahead of benefits.

(4) The original insurance scheme was intended to embody actuarial principles, i.e. the benefits were related to the contributions and as everybody paid the same contributions (according to sex) everybody received the same amount of benefit. As has been shown in the last chapter, unemployment benefit was forced by circumstances to alter. Dependants' allowances were introduced as a temporary measure and it was confidently assumed that it would soon be possible to return to the original plan; but mass unemployment lasted so long that this time never arrived and by the end of the thirties the great value of dependants' allowances had become so obvious that, instead of getting rid of them, the Health Insurance scheme was bitterly criticized for not including them. The new scheme therefore included dependants' allowances as an essential part of the benefits.

(5) The benefits continue very much longer than in the old scheme—in most cases as long as the situation requiring them lasts. But there are certain conditions regarding the contributions that have to be met. Sickness benefit is not paid for more than a year unless at least 156 contributions (i.e. three years' worth) have been made and unemployment benefit is paid, in the first instance, for 30 weeks, though it may be continued up to nineteen months in all, if sufficient contributions have been paid in the preceding period.

(6) Retirement Pensions have replaced Old Age Pensions.

The Old Age Pension could be claimed by a man who reached 65 years of age and a woman who reached 60, whether they continued in work or not. Retirement Pensions, as the name implies, are paid when work has been given up. They can be claimed at 65 for a man and 60 for a woman, providing any work done does not bring in more than a certain amount, but they are intended for those who have retired. On the other hand, anybody who goes on working after 65 and 60 can later claim a larger retirement pension when they *do* give up according to the length of the period they have remained at work.

(7) The Industrial Injuries scheme has replaced Workmen's Compensation. By the old system an injured workman had a civil claim against his employer and had to uphold it, if necessary, in the courts. But even if his claim proved valid he was not sure of any compensation, for his employer might have omitted to insure against this liability and be insolvent. The Industrial Injuries scheme is an insurance system like the others, and like them is financed by three-sided contributions from employers, workers and the State, so there is no fear that funds will not be available, if it can be shown that the injury was suffered in the course of employment.

One might ask why, in this case, should it not be included in the sickness insurance and this, indeed, would have been the logical course. There was a difficulty, however. Workmen's Compensation did not provide the absolute security of help that had been intended, but once a man had made good his claim and if he also had a solvent employer to pay it, the amount he got was considerably more than the benefits under sickness insurance. There would have been serious opposition to any attempt to drop these rates to bring them into line with sickness benefit and the only alternative was to have a separate scheme.

(8) All these benefits are now administered by one authority, the Ministry of Social Security. The Approved Societies, of the old Health Insurance scheme, for example, have been abandoned and now every insured person has the same rights to benefit.

(9) Whatever the insurance schemes may be, there are always individual circumstances that do not fit exactly within the prescribed definitions. Some people may require more than the legal benefits provided or they may need other than monetary help, or they may exhaust their rights and still not have recovered from their particular difficulty. Some service that can take account of these individual circumstances is, therefore, essential if the community is to fulfil its responsibility of seeing that none of its members falls below the accepted minimum standard of living. The National Assistance Act, 1948, which abolished the old Poor Law provides this final service. It is now administered by the Ministry of Social Security and is financed entirely out of public funds, i.e. taxation.

Beyond insurance

The National Assistance Board deals with many more than those who have exhausted their insurance rights or who find them insufficient. It has the duty of providing for everybody in need whatever the cause, whose need is not provided for by some other statutory scheme; for example, the wife and children of a prisoner or of a man who has deserted his family, or old people who were too old to be included in the Retirement Pension system; in fact, anybody who finds himself in financial difficulties with the one exception that the National Assistance Board may not supplement the wages of people in full-time employment. As this is an individual service and depends on the particular financial difficulty in which the individual person finds himself a needs test is essential, but this test is a purely personal one. The law lays an obligation on a man or woman to support their spouse and young children, so this is the only source of help from relatives that the needs test takes into account. The Board lays down a national scale of the sums to be paid and the resources of the individual that may be calculated in estimating his need (and on the whole, his needs are assessed generously) though additional amounts may be paid in certain circumstances as, for example, to pay for domestic help for an infirm old person and so on.

The Act expressly requires the officers of the Board 'to exercise their functions in such a manner as shall best promote the welfare of the persons affected, that is the welfare of the persons assisted and their dependants' and this statutory duty has had an immense influence in changing the whole attitude to national assistance. Instead of trying to deter people from asking for help, as did the old Poor Law, the NAB positively *urges* people who may be in need to apply to them and much effort is expended in searching out those who may be shy about doing so.

The main duty of the Board is to provide financial help in order to maintain a minimum standard of income but it has another important duty. This is to provide homes and welfare services for the aged and the handicapped, and here the general trend has been to substitute small home-like hostels with many social amenities and pleasant furnishings and equipment, for the large, forbidding, barrack-like institutions that were common earlier.

Provision for dependents

All these schemes provide an income for periods when, for one reason or another, the individual is unable to earn enough to meet his obligations and all, in a sense, are developments of the original system of compulsory national insurance against common risks. But there was one Act which broke new ground for it provided an addition to income even during earning. This was the Family Allowances Act, 1945.

The long period of mass unemployment between the two wars brought out very clearly the heavy burden on the wage earner during the time when his young family was entirely dependent on his wages. That a family man has heavier essential expenses than a bachelor or a childless couple had long been recognized with regard to higher incomes, i.e. those which were high enough to come within the scope of the Income Tax; and before PAYE was invented in 1940 this was a very small minority of the population. The family man could claim that allowance be made in his assessment for the fact that he had a wife and children to maintain; but as practically no wage earners earned enough to pay income tax no allowances were made for the family responsibilities that they had to meet.

When dependants' allowances were introduced into unemployment benefit there was a real dilemma. An unskilled labourer with several children could get a larger weekly sum when out of work than he could get when employed, for wages do not and, of course, cannot take into account the size of a man's family. But this dilemma threw a glaring light on the problem of the lower paid worker with a young family.

The Family Allowances Act was passed to deal with this difficulty. It provides a weekly income out of taxation in respect of every child other than the first as long as the child is at school. There is no means test and the allowance is paid to every family irrespective of its resources; but, of course, as it is included in the total income calculated for income tax, richer people pay a good deal of it back as tax.

The legislation discussed so far has the aim of ensuring to every individual a minimum standard of income and care; but it is in the other elements of welfare, apart from income, that the greatest achievements have been made since the thirties—education, health and housing—and it is to these that we must now turn our attention.

(ii) Education

Beveridge's second demand was for a good education system and the developments in this field are amongst the most important that have taken place during the last two decades. Compulsory education at elementary schools was introduced in 1870 though it was not until 1890 that it became free. The minimum school leaving age was then 13 though children were permitted to leave earlier or to attend only half-time in certain circumstances. In the early years of the twentieth century the school leaving age was raised to 14, part time was abolished and a system of secondary or grammar schools was established under the control of local education authorities. Every secondary school maintained out of public funds was bound to offer a proportion of 'free places' and a system of scholarships open to competition enabled the most able children to continue their education even if their parents could not afford the fees; but, for the most part, grammar schools were for the middle classes and the large majority of the children of wage earners had to be content with the education they received at the elementary schools up to the age of 14.

There had been much criticism of this situation between the two wars and many committees had deliberated and made recommendations. There was much condemnation of an educational system which shut the door in the face of a clever child because his parents could not afford to pay for him or were unaware of the importance of continued schooling. And there was also much fear of the cost to the community of the waste of so much potential talent.

The Education Act, 1944, was an attempt to change this situation radically. The school leaving age was raised to 15 but, more important, the whole set-up of educational provision was reorganized. The new system was based on three stages: (*a*) primary from the age of 5 to 11 plus, (*b*) secondary from 11 plus, (*c*) further education and higher education to include part-time and full-time education after the secondary

20. *The type of school we are building now*

stage. As the aim of the Act was to provide education suited to the ability of the pupil, secondary schools, which now became free to all, were divided into three types which were thought to correspond to different kinds of ability and interest. Grammar schools were planned for those of the highest intellectual ability, secondary modern schools for those of a less intellectual turn of mind and technical secondary schools for those with a particular practical bent who would be likely later to go into some form of skilled manual occupation. Since the Act came into operation there has been constant criticism of the three-fold secondary stage. It is argued that it is not possible to make a fair selection of intellectual ability at such an early age and that the knowledge that his whole future life will be determined by an examination at that time has a serious effect on the pupil and increases family tensions in the home. Many local education authorities are attempting to get over the difficulty by substituting comprehensive schools at the secondary stage which provide the various types of course to suit different kinds of capacity and interest in the one school.

School Welfare Services

Well-planned schools to fit different types of ability are, however, not the only needs of a good educational system. Children who are ill or underfed, or suffering from an emotional disturbance cannot take advantage of the schooling offered them and as early as 1906 the Education (Provision of Meals) Act empowered local education authorities to provide milk and meals for elementary school children who were unable to learn because they were suffering from malnutrition.

From this modest beginning great developments have taken place, partly because of the special needs thrown up by the Second World War. Women were urged to help the war effort and mothers who were in the factories could not provide meals at home. Good food for children—however strict the rationing of adults—was considered an absolute essential and therefore the School Meals Service was extended to fill the need. Milk at low cost was distributed at the morning and afternoon breaks and schools were urged to accept the provision of canteens giving hot dinners as a normal part of their equipment and function. Now close on two-thirds of children in grant-aided schools take these meals—whether free of charge or for payment—and more than four-fifths take advantage of the 'milk in schools' scheme.

This alone has had an enormous influence on health but it has been aided by the School Medical Service started in 1908 which has now grown into a very comprehensive Schools Health Service. Routine inspections are made and supplementary examinations whenever a teacher or a parent suspects there may be some condition needing treatment. How much of the greatly improved standard of health and cleanliness of school children is due to these two services and how much to the higher standards of living in the community generally it is difficult to judge; but there is no doubt at all of the immense contribution they have made.

As higher education

As important as the development of free secondary education has been the growing provision for higher education, both in the universities and in technical colleges and colleges of further education. At the beginning of the present century the only institutions for higher education were the universities and for the most part their students were drawn from the upper and middle classes. Most of the sons of the highest social strata went to a university as part of their social, as much as their intellectual, education and those of the middle classes who entered did so to prepare themselves for professional occupations or high managerial posts. The great changes that have taken place have been both in the number and kinds of institutions of higher learning and in the students who attend them. Training Colleges (for the training of teachers, now called Colleges of Education), Institutes of Education, Technical Colleges, Colleges of Advanced Technology, Colleges of Commerce, Schools of Art have been set up in addition to the expansion of the existing universities and the foundation of new ones. Those which provide full-time instruction no longer favour the rich or even the exceptionally able; but, as part of the new provision of educational facilities to suit the ability of the individual, any person who has the intellectual capacity to get a place in one of these is assured of an allowance from public funds which is sufficient to pay his fees and his maintenance. In addition to these there has been an enormous expansion in part-time courses attended by those in employment, which enable them to take the qualifications which lead to promotion in their particular field.

Despite this great expansion of educational opportunity it is still true, however, that the proportion of students in these institutions coming from wage-earning homes is much less than one would expect considering the proportion of such families in the population. It is not because of the lack of opportunity nor because of any bias in selection (as has been shown by a careful comparison of the social origins of those selected and those rejected) but because there are, as yet, large sections of the community who are unwilling to take advantage of the facilities offered. To a certain extent this may be due to fear of the unknown. A boy or girl born into a family in which no member has remained at school beyond the age of 14 or 15 may be afraid of venturing forth on uncharted seas; to some extent it may be due to the lack of encouragement at home or even to positive discouragement and unwillingness to allow privacy for study; or the comparison with friends in the neighbourhood who are already earning good wages may be a real obstacle. If so, all these are likely to be less effective in the future as wage-earning families become more familiar with the possibilities of higher education and the able child who goes on after the legal school-leaving age becomes less of a rarity.

Training for employment

Most of these new developments have been concerned to give opportunities to those who have the willingness and ability to continue their education beyond the legal minimum school-leaving age. But what of the others? Four-fifths of the school population leave full-time education within a year of this age and go into employment. What happens to them?

Until very recently this has been an unhappy story. Almost immediately after the Labour Exchanges were set up in 1909 a special Juvenile Department was established; for it was realized that placing young people in jobs is very different from dealing with adults. As far as adults are concerned the problem is one of matching workers who have certain skills or experience with employers who have vacancies; but school leavers have not yet acquired industrial skill or experience. They need help in choosing the field of employment into which to go in the knowledge that their choices will probably affect the rest of their lives. It is not enough for those who advise them to know something of the interests and aptitudes of the child; they must also have some knowledge of the likely trends that industry will show. For example, it would have been little use to have advised a youngster who was keen on horses to become the driver of a horse-drawn cab, say, about thirty years ago when motor cars were beginning to take over.

Because of this twofold task there has always been controversy as to whether young people should be advised by the Ministry of Labour, which knows a lot about industry, or by the Ministry of Education,* which knows more about young people; and until 1948 the division of function between them meant that neither did the work properly. Since the Employment and Training Act of that year, however, there has been a great advance. The division remains but as both are subject to a central executive on which both are represented, the special knowledge of both can be mobilized and good standards maintained, irrespective of which authority actually runs the service. As a general thing, the local education authorities are responsible for the Youth Employment Service in the urban areas and the Ministry of Labour in the rural ones; but there are, of course, some exceptions to this general rule.

* Now the Department of Education and Science.

Whichever authority undertakes the work it is under the supervision of the Central Youth Employment Executive which provides a great deal of information for Youth Employment Officers, and for young people, their teachers and parents, and which is constantly trying to improve the standard of assistance which is given to young people in their choice of jobs.

Finding a job is not difficult. Ever since the end of the Second World War there have almost always been more openings than young people to fill them (except in one or two areas where the main industry has been declining); but finding a job with a future is an entirely different matter for this depends on opportunities for training. And it is here that the story so far has not been so happy.

Traditionally the training of people for employment has always been considered the responsibility of the employers and the State has played very little part in it. Industry has always made a clear dividing line between skilled trades for

21. *A Youth Employment Officer with a school-leaver and his mother*

which an apprenticeship is required and all the other kinds of jobs. In fact, the dividing line is nothing like so definite as has been assumed. Most jobs, if they are to be done well, require some amount of learning or experience and, in practice, there is a whole range of skill from the lowest to the highest; but this has unfortunately been ignored, and only the highest kinds of skilled manual work have had specific training.

Apprenticeship regulations are not controlled by the State; they are the subject of voluntary collective agreements between the employers and the trade unions in the trade concerned; but although each trade makes its own agreements there is a strong family resemblance between all the schemes. They all last five years,* beginning at 16 and ending at 21; none of them admits apprentices at a later age or for a shorter period except on rare occasions; they all lay down the curriculum to be followed so as to ensure a comprehensive experience of all the processes in the trade and they all contain agreements that apprentices shall be released for one day a week, without loss of pay, up to the eighteenth birthday to attend theoretical classes at a local Technical College or College of Further Education. This technical instruction, which is provided free of charge as part of the normal educational facilities is the only respect in which the State plays a part in training the young for their future employment.

There are a very large number of such collectively agreed schemes but many trades have only a small group of skilled workers to be affected by them. Indeed, two-thirds of all skilled men are found in one small group of industries—engineering in all its branches, shipbuilding, printing, building and construction and motor repair and maintenance—though these between them employ a very large number of people.

Of all the boys who leave school just over one-third go into apprenticeships but only 5 to 6% of girls. This is because most girls expect to be married by the time they are 21 or soon after and are unwilling to spend five years in training for

* The building industry has recently reduced this period to four years.

a job they are unlikely to practise; and employers are not too eager to get them to change their minds when they know that so much of their training will be wasted.

The Industrial Training Act of 1964

What happens to the remainder? Until a few years ago it would have been impossible to answer this question for there are no national agreements covering the training of non-apprentices. Recently, however, the Ministry of Labour began to collect information on training schemes that had been introduced by individual firms. It asked for details of any courses of instruction that lasted at least eight weeks and from these enquiries it appears that 15% of boys and 13% of girls receive at least this modest amount of training. If we add these to the number of apprentices we find that about 50% of boys and 19% of girls get at least eight weeks training. Looked at from the opposite angle this means that half the boys and nearly four-fifths of the girls do not get even eight weeks help in making the transfer from school to work.

This transfer is one of the biggest breaks to be made in life. There is first the change in the number of hours of the working day, from 5½ to 8 or even more, quite apart from the time that may have to be spent in travelling. At school the pupil is the centre of attention; the curriculum is planned for his benefit, there are frequent breaks for meals and recreation and the teachers are there to help him to understand and to encourage him to learn. At work, all is different. He is an unimportant part of the work team, constantly getting under the feet of impatient adults; the jobs are strange and often seem meaningless, but there is nobody there to explain them to him or show him the best way to do them. And this big change is made at a time when he has to learn to be independent, when he is conscious of becoming a grown-up in an adult world and when he is coping with the many emotional and biological problems of adolescence.

Even the apprentice who comes into one of the agreed schemes cannot be sure of a good training for although the regulations seem to ensure a thorough grounding in all aspects of his trade there is no certainty that he will receive this or that his employer will release him to attend the technical classes. The regulations are agreed but there is no way of enforcing them. Some firms take their training responsibilities very seriously and have well-thought out and supervised schemes; but these unhappily are in a minority. Many take no interest in their apprentices and do not even bother to move them from process to process to see that they learn all the various parts of the trade, and do not honour their obligation to release them for the theoretical classes. Even in the very good firms it is rare to find anybody whose job it is to see that the apprentice gets taught his job; he is expected to pick it up by watching others.

What proportion of apprentices do manage to learn to do their jobs properly we have no means of knowing for there are no tests of competence. At the end of the five-year term the young man is considered a skilled worker whether he has learned anything or not. He may have been kept all the time at one process on which his employer found him specially useful; he may never have attended a class; or have failed to understand what he was taught if he did; but he is still considered a fully skilled man and must be paid the rate of wages for that grade.

This lack of standards in training is not the only problem; there is also a very serious shortage of skilled workers. This is due to the fact that many firms are no longer willing to take apprentices at all and though this is found mainly amongst the small and medium sized firms it is by no means confined to them. Apprentices used to be a source of profit to firms for not only were the wages very low but in many cases parents had to pay a premium to induce firms to take their sons. All this has changed. Premiums are a thing of the past and apprentices' wages are now a proportion of the adult skilled rate and go up year by year; and if the firm releases the youth one day a week to attend classes this wage is being paid for only four days' work.

The smaller firms have added difficulties to cope with. The absence of the apprentice upsets the work schedule of the team with which he is working (bigger firms can organize to overcome this) and, moreover, the present tendency towards increased specialization means that many small firms no longer do a comprehensive series of jobs but only carry out specialized parts of large jobs.

This persistent shortage of skilled workers has been one of the greatest handicaps with which the British economy has been faced during the last twenty years. It leads to long delays in production, not only in the skilled trades themselves but in all the others which are held up waiting for machine tools or key parts. It also leads to great resentment because firms which have given up training completely entice away the skilled men trained by others.

The Industrial Training Act passed in 1964 is an attempt to deal with all these problems. It marks the beginning of a new epoch for this is the first time that the State has accepted responsibility for industrial training. In a sense it is the second half of the Education Act, 1944, in that it tries to see that those who go into industry instead of staying on at school also have an opportunity to develop their abilities.

The Act does not lay down the specific training that people should have any more than the Education Acts tell schools what to teach; but it sets up the machinery for teaching. Instead of contenting itself with urging industry to take care of its young recruits it lays down certain duties which must be fulfilled, though there are various ways in which they can be carried out.

Under the Act the Minister of Labour will set up for every industry an Industrial Training Board composed of equal numbers of representatives of employers and workers and also of a number of educationalists. These Boards have certain compulsory duties and certain powers they may use. Each Board must ensure that adequate training is provided for all grades of workers (not only the highly skilled) and must publish their recommendations of the nature, content and length of the training and of the further education associated with it. These recommendations are effective for the other main duty of the Boards is to make every firm in the industry pay a levy whether it does any training or not; but, on the other hand, any firm may apply to the Board for a grant which will be paid if its training is at least as good as the standards laid down. This 'levy and grant' system is the most important part of the new scheme for it ensures:

(*a*) that the training curriculum is actually followed,

(*b*) that the training is open to inspection,

(*c*) that firms which do no training have to contribute towards the expenses of those that do.

The Minister of Labour has announced that he will not approve any scheme which does not include provision for Day Release and this means that there is at last some compulsion on employers, at least on those who apply for grant, to allow their younger workers to attend classes at the Colleges of Further Education.

During recent years there have been some very successful experiments in organizing full-time courses of instruction for the first year of training in which both the practical work and the theoretical teaching are carefully combined. The apprentices attending such courses have very rapidly learned the remaining processes when they entered the workshop for productive work because they had gained a real understanding of the jobs involved. The Boards that have been set up seem very likely to specify this period of 'off the job' training as one of the essentials in any scheme which is to qualify for a grant (this has already been announced by the Engineering Training Board). Moreover, there is a trend to make this first basic instruction much more general than apprenticeship schemes have been up to now. This in itself will do much to improve the character of the training and to reduce the shortage of skilled workers. The rapidity of technological change is now so great that in the future it will be the exception rather than the rule for a man to be in the same trade throughout his working life and only those who are not too narrowly specialized are able to adapt themselves to new techniques.

The Minister of Labour has a Central Training Council to advise him on all matters connected with training and this has undertaken a number of functions that are important to all occupations whichever Industrial Training Board they come under. For example, every industry must have a number of employees in commercial and clerical occupations and these need training as much as those doing the manufacturing processes; so a committee of the Central Training Council works out suitable forms of training which each separate board will be advised to prescribe. Similarly, the training of instructors and research into the best methods of teaching workshop practice are subjects undertaken by the Council because these are matters of importance to all.

(iii) Health

The health insurance scheme of 1911 was designed to do two things: (1) to provide some income for a wage earner who was unable to work because of illness, and (2) to provide him with medical attention. Doctors were paid according to their number of patients, and insured people could choose to have their name put on the panel or list of any doctor who agreed to take part in the scheme. In this way all the working population, for the first time in their lives, could be sure of receiving skilled help during sickness. Some could get a good deal more, for the variety of services offered depended on the wealth of the Approved Society to which the insured person belonged. But however rich and well run an Approved Society might be it covered only its members and there was no service to look after their wives and children. Apart from insured working men the large majority of the population never saw a doctor because they could not afford the fees. We are now very familiar with the term 'the family doctor' but, in fact, in the early years of this century such an idea was unknown and it is doubtful if more than 10 to 20% of the population who had to pay a fee ever consulted a doctor at all.

Hospitals

Medical care in the home is, of course, not all that is needed to care for the sick. For many illnesses and for all operations a hospital service is required and there were until recently two distinct hospital systems—the voluntary hospital and the municipal. The first of these, many of which were very old charities like St Thomas's and Barts, could trace their history back to the Middle Ages and were independent organizations which relied on endowments and subscriptions for their funds. They varied greatly both in size and efficiency. Some of them were very large with the latest equipment and distinguished consultants on their staff and included outstanding medical schools which student doctors competed to enter; others were tiny hospitals in a small country town served by local general practitioners. Much of a patient's chances of recovery depended on which hospital he was able to enter for treatment.

22. *A new hospital building. Guy's Hospital's new surgical block rises above the old buildings of the neighbourhood*

The municipal hospitals were the responsibility of the local authority. They had originally been part of the provision of the poor law when the duty of caring for the sick poor was part of the functions of the Boards of Guardians. As has been shown in an earlier chapter, they had at first been solely for the destitute but as their standards improved they were used more and more by those who would never have dreamed of applying, or have needed to apply, to the Boards of Guardians for help. When the Boards of Guardians were abolished in 1929 and their poor relief duties were vested in the local authorities it became an accepted principle that the local authorities should provide hospitals for the use of all and not only for the destitute.

Both voluntary and municipal hospitals had developed in a haphazard way; and there was nothing to ensure that sick people in need of a hospital would be fortunate enough to find one in the locality in which they lived. The seriousness of this lack was becoming more evident on account of the great strides in medical knowledge and practice made during the present century. Increasing understanding of the factors in illness—both physical and mental—made people less ready than they had been before to have recourse to 'old wives' remedies' and there was an ever growing demand for trained medical attention and careful nursing. With rising standards of living and more awareness of the causes of disease, people were less willing to accept illness as one of the 'natural' misfortunes of life to be borne with fortitude but without doing much about it. It was recognized that much suffering could be avoided if illness could be diagnosed at an early stage and if careful treatment were available. There was, therefore, a strong case for a thorough reorganization of the provision for dealing with sickness, as an essential element in increasing the welfare of society.

The Health Service

The National Health Service Act, 1946, was the result. In its own words its object is 'to promote the establishment in

England and Wales (there are similar acts for Scotland and Northern Ireland) of a comprehensive service designed to secure improvement in the physical and mental health of the people of England and Wales and the prevention, diagnosis and treatment of illness, and for that purpose to secure the effective provision of services'. Originally the services were free of charge to all members of the community, according to medical need, without regard to any insurance contribution. The money to finance the scheme is drawn from general taxation with the exception of a small contribution from the weekly payments made by insured people to the National Insurance Fund. At different times, however, certain charges have been demanded for particular parts of the service. For example, a small basic payment must now be paid for spectacles because it was believed that people treated these fragile articles rather too lightheartedly when they knew they could always be replaced without any cost to themselves. Similarly, there is always much political wrangling on whether there should, or should not be, a charge for prescriptions. Some argue that complete freedom leads to waste and an increased demand for the free provision of some common remedies that most households usually keep in their own cupboards to treat minor ills such as headaches and scratches. Others contend that any charge cuts across the principle of the Health Service and bears particularly heavily on families with children who, in any case, find difficulty in making ends meet. The Labour Party, when it came into office in 1964, for instance, abolished the prescription charge of 2*s*. that had been imposed by its predessor, the Conservative Government, and thus added £40 millions to the annual cost of the service to be met out of taxation.

The Health Service falls into three parts:

(1) The general practitioner services. These include the family doctors, dentists, the eye service and the pharmaceutical service. They are administered by over 160 local executive councils on which doctors, dentists and pharmacists are represented. Doctors and dentists are not compelled to take part in the service but, in fact, almost all choose to do so.

Doctors are paid according to the number on their list (patients can choose the doctor to whom they wish to be attached) but no doctor may have more than 3,500 names on his list and in practice the average is somewhere around 2,300. Dentists are paid according to the actual treatments they give.

It is usually through their doctors that patients get most other services, e.g. ophthalmic and specialist treatment.

(2) The hospital and specialist services. These are administered through 20 Regional Hospital Boards and nearly 500 hospital management committees, all of which are under the authority of the Minister of Health. The aim is to allow for experiment and flexibility and to create a sense of local loyalty and responsibility; but at times the Minister may issue general instructions so as to maintain certain standards and to prevent too great a difference in the services offered.

The hospitals, of which there are about 3,000, provide general and specialist care—for both in-patients and out-patients. Some of the staff are full-time and receive salaries from the National Health Service; others are part-time and are paid according to how often they attend, and also have a private practice, for whilst the Service is free to all there is no compulsion on patients to make use of it.

Hospitals recognize that patients come from widely differing home backgrounds and that too great a change from customary ways of living may make recovery slower. A limited number of 'amenity' beds may, therefore, be put aside for those wishing for privacy provided that they are not needed on medical grounds by non-paying patients. The charges for these are fixed by statutory regulations. In some hospitals there is also provision for private patients who are being treated by their own doctors but in this case the charge must cover the full cost of accommodation and care.

(3) The local authority services consist of maternity and child welfare, services for the prevention of illness, home visiting, health visiting, home nursing, domestic help, ambulance services and so on. These are administered by the larger local authorities.

This thoroughgoing reorganization of hospital and medical

service could not be made without a good deal of controversy and some difficulty. It involved a very great change in the attitudes of all concerned. It is no easy matter for a doctor who has been, as it were, a law unto himself, subservient only to his Hippocratic oath,* to find himself compelled to work within a framework of regulations, to have forms to fill in, to be bound to answer the criticisms of various authorities and so on; nor has it been easy for hospitals to fit their organization into a large national scheme. And certainly there are patients who have abused their rights and demanded an undue amount of attention for minor troubles from harassed and overworked doctors or have wanted attention at highly inconvenient times. But there is no doubt that the National Health Service, despite its complexity, very quickly got into working order and has proved itself one of the most valuable parts of the Welfare State.

(iv) Housing

The State provision of schools and hospitals for the use of its citizens presents no great difficulty once the policy has been decided. Few individuals are rich enough to build such institutions for their own use and experience has shown that only a minority can afford to pay enough for their use to make it worth while for profit making companies to erect and maintain them. So if the community wants them they must, of necessity, be provided by communal effort. But housing is in quite a different category. Everybody needs somewhere to live—not at special times as with hospitals, nor during a limited period, as with schools, but throughout one's life. It can be assumed, therefore, that everybody recognizes this as one of the needs that must be met out of one's resources, whatever else one sacrifices to do so. Why, then, should the State play any part in this?

* The oath of service to his patients and the principles of his profession taken by each doctor on qualifying. Named after Hippocrates, the Greek 'Founder' of medicine.

The most obvious reason is that the lack of cleanliness or facilities for waste disposal in one house may have serious effects on the health of other people living in the neighbourhood and, indeed, the first housing Acts were primarily concerned with establishing and maintaining standards of hygiene, through water supply, sewerage, drainage, etc. But there are other less obvious reasons for public concern.

(1) A building generally lasts a long time but needs constant expenditure on repairs and maintenance. Pipes rust and break, roof tiles fall off and admit the rain, window frames get warped, ceilings and floors sag, plaster must be renewed and so on. Unless the landlord knows that the tenant's rent will cover these costs he is unwilling to incur them. Thus whole areas fall into disrepair and become slums, the only cure for which is complete evacuation and rebuilding—a very expensive process.

(2) Standards of housing constantly change, both as a result of different ideas of what is acceptable in a community and on account of new developments in industry. For example, at one time nobody, not even the very rich, had running water or flush lavatories because these had not yet been invented. When they were, the rich could afford to have them installed, and, as new houses were built, they were introduced as standard equipment. Thus the older houses, which had been a good average quality before, fell lower and lower in the social scale and were let out as tenements, room by room, without any of the kitchen and bathroom equipment needed by the families forced by their low wages to occupy them.

This is a continuous process. Houses built today have fittings that were unheard of even ten years ago, except for the homes built to sell or let at very high rates.

(3) In a system of private enterprise, such as exists in most of the western world, it is understood that you cannot have things for which you are unwilling or unable to pay. If, for example, the price of tobacco or beer goes up, you know you have to be content to smoke and drink less; and even when food prices rise you content yourself with more of the cheaper

23. *New Council housing*

and less of the dearer foods. But a home is different. You must either pay the rent or get out and to be turned out of your house is much more serious than reducing your consumption of cigarettes or food. But however vital it may be to the tenant to remain in the house, the rent he gets for his house is the landlord's income and, like every other producer, he charges what he can get. Rent is the same as every other price; it goes up when there is scarcity because there is a bigger demand; or when the costs of production rise and it is more expensive to make.

During the present century both these factors have played a big part. During the two world wars the building of houses was restricted because the men and materials were needed for the war and, as the population was increasing, the end of each war saw an enormous upsurge in the demand for homes. But at the same time, the standard of housing required rose sharply. People were not content with the type of house that had been customary before. They wanted more rooms per family, better construction and a much higher type of fittings for kitchens and bathrooms; so the cost of producing houses and flats has gone up, and unless rents go up too it is not worth while for producers to build them. Therefore, if the community thinks it is necessary for people to be able to live in dwellings of a certain standard it must take some part in ensuring that they are built.

(4) With improved communications it is no longer necessary for people to live very close to their work. With trams, buses, trains, bicycles and cars available they spread out to new suburbs and this leaves the old residential areas in the centre of the towns to become derelict. At the same time, the country is increasingly urbanized and access to green fields and fresh air becomes more difficult. It thus comes to be essential to control the siting of the new houses—both to protect the countryside and to prevent the constant lengthening of the working day by long journeys.

All these matters have contributed to the housing policy of the present century—the control of rents, local authority building, the planning of building zones and green belts, the clearance of slums, the building of housing estates and the setting up of complete New Towns.

State provision of housing

It was not until the end of the First World War that this positive stage in policy began. Then the Government accepted responsibility for enforcing minimum standards of housing construction, for encouraging slum clearance and for new building by paying subsidies to local authorities to persuade them to undertake the work. It thus became possible to build houses of a much higher standard than before the war to let to working class tenants at a rent which was considerably below their economic value. The amount and terms of the subsidies have varied from time to time according to the Government's estimates of varying needs and to different political pressures. The latest Act is that of 1961 which provides subsidies in respect of all approved dwellings built by local authorities, Housing Associations and New Towns and it is estimated that now two-thirds of all the houses built since the end of the Second World War have been built by public authority. In addition, private owners can obtain assistance from public funds for the improvement and reconditioning of houses built before 1945 or to convert large houses which are now too big for single family occupation.

Despite this big increase in the part played by the State in the provision of housing there are still many unsolved problems:

(1) The father of a large family finds it difficult to pay the rent of a house big enough to accommodate all his children even though it is subsidized. Some local authorities have introduced rent rebates, i.e. they charge a rent which takes into account the income of the tenant and the number of his dependants. But many authorities are unwilling to do this partly because they believe it to be unfair to charge different rents for similar accommodation, and partly because they dislike administering a means test.

(2) The very long periods during which strict rent control

was in operation had two serious consequences: (*a*) many houses fell into bad repair because their owners could not afford to invest capital in their reconditioning when the returns they received as rent were so low; (*b*) as wages rose the rent paid by tenants came to represent a very small proportion of their weekly expenditure—very much lower than in most other industrial countries. People became so accustomed to this that any increase in rent involved a big alteration in their budgeting and this aroused much resentment. Yet unless houses are to be let at rents that represent their economic cost there can be no chance of private builders supplementing the building by local authorities. This has caused a real dilemma.

(3) Mobility of labour is one of the essentials of a flexible progressive economy; but one of the greatest hindrances to movement is the fear that one may not be able to rent a house within one's means in the place where work is available.

(4) Most local authorities give preference on their housing lists to those with young children; but as the years pass the children grow up and move away. The parents are left with a house too big for their needs whilst young families are still unable to find a home. What should be done? Should the older people be forced to move? On the one hand they cling to their homes in the familiar neighbourhood which is near to their friends and want to have space for their married children to visit them. On the other, should public funds be used to subsidize their rents when other families are in greater need? Or sometimes it happens that a family with an income which justified a subsidized rent when the house was first allocated to them, later earns a much bigger income—higher than many other families still on the waiting list. Should they be forced to make way for others when they are no longer in need?

(5) When slums are cleared the alternative accommodation offered is often at a distance—on a new housing estate or in a New Town. The new home is more comfortable and more up-to-date but the people in it are cut off from old friends and the other members of the family. This is not only a loss

in social and friendly intercourse but it makes almost impossible all the informal help that members of a family give one another—shopping for granny when the weather is bad, baby-sitting for a daughter or sister, providing meals for the children when the mother is ill and so on.

(v) Pictures, plays and music

One very new responsibility has been undertaken by the Welfare State since the end of the Second World War—that is, to encourage the production and the appreciation of cultural activities. Just as with other social services this has been founded on the experimental work done by a voluntary body. As early as 1935 'Art for the People' was established by W. E. Williams (now Sir William Emrys Williams, C.B.E., D.Litt.) to persuade private owners of pictures and sculpture to lend some of their possessions for months at a time so that travelling exhibitions could be sent to small towns and villages whose inhabitants had never before had an opportunity to see an original work of art. The next step was taken at the outbreak of war when CEMA—the Committee for the Encouragement of Music and the Arts—was set up with a dual purpose: to help practising artists to continue their work and to give the community the opportunity to enjoy concerts and pictures despite the stress of war.

The Government and the Pilgrim Trust (a privately endowed foundation) provided funds to enable CEMA to carry out these tasks and so valuable did this work prove to be that as soon as the war was over the Arts Council of Great Britain was founded to allow the work to develop on a permanent basis. The Arts Council draws all its funds from the Government and has the duty of deciding which ventures to support, in order to encourage and maintain high standards in the production of art of all forms and to spread the appreciation and enjoyment of the arts in the community.

In carrying out these functions the Arts Council subsidizes the operas produced by Covent Garden and Sadlers Wells, the principal orchestras, a great many theatres all over the country, the Festivals of the Arts, the mounting of special exhibitions of pictures and sculpture and a travelling exhibition of works of art in its own possession. As a result, operas, concerts, plays, etc., etc., can be put on which would be beyond the means of commercial companies and hundreds of thousands of people have an opportunity to see them at prices they can afford to pay.

Since 1948 there has been a further development. The Local Government Act of that year authorized local authorities to levy up to a *6d.* rate to provide funds for similar purposes within their boundaries. Many of them have taken advantage of this permission—notably London with its Royal Festival Hall—and help to finance civic theatres and orchestras and so on.

5. PROBLEMS FOR THE FUTURE

What of the future? Is the Welfare State complete? By no means.

Every generation has to solve afresh for itself the problems set by the vicissitudes of human life because each generation begins, as it were, from a different point and with different ideas. Few people nowadays hold the belief (as most did in the nineteenth century) that it is wrong for the State to interfere in order to try to better the general conditions of the mass of the population. Most now accept that the State has a responsibility for the welfare of its members and that there are many circumstances in which this cannot be achieved except by public action. But this does not mean that everybody is unanimous on where to draw the line between social and individual responsibility; nor does it mean that we all agree on the means to be used even when we agree where the main responsibility should lie.

In the earlier part of this century it was assumed that help was needed only by those who, for one reason or another, fell below the accepted standard of living; and all the earlier schemes tried to define these groups and to devise methods for supporting them without destroying individual initiative and resourcefulness. So laws were framed to assist the weaker sections of the community (Factory Acts, Public Health Acts, Trade Boards Acts, Labour Exchanges, etc.) or to provide a solid footing on which personal effort could be built (Insurance schemes). It was assumed that the rest of the community could easily make its own arrangements and should be left to do so.

Then came the long period of chronic mass unemployment between the two wars. The percentage of the insured population who were out of work dropped below 10% only for two short periods and twice it was well over 20%. The numbers of wage-earners and lower grades of clerical workers who were victims of the depression could be counted because of their insurance claims, the others could not. But we could be certain that if such a large proportion of the insured were without work there must be thousands of businesses that had gone bankrupt or which could barely keep themselves solvent, and that thousands of business men, technicians, managers and higher-grade workers were in distress. We could no longer take it for granted, therefore, that financial difficulty was a problem confined to the 'working classes' whilst all the rest had a secure standard of living. So when Beveridge planned his schemes he stressed their 'all-in' character and devised the new system to include practically the whole community.

Rising expectations

In the twenty years or so since the Beveridge Report was published ideas have changed again. We have had a long period of growing wealth, with rapidly changing techniques of production and new inventions which have greatly altered our ways of living. Unemployment has been very slight, we are much richer than we were and we have grown accustomed to the use of all sorts of things as a commonplace in our homes, and leisure times that we had hardly heard of before. As a result, our idea of what constitutes a basic subsistence has altered. Not only do we include amongst the 'necessities of life' many things that were earlier thought of as luxuries, but we recognize that there is no such thing as an absolute 'minimum standard of living'. We are no longer content to calculate the lowest cost of keeping a family alive (as did Booth and Rowntree) but we believe that this minimum is a relative idea, rising as we grow richer, and that therefore, the assured basis must go up as the general standards of living of the whole population improve. Our targets today are therefore different from those of our fathers.

There is another way in which our ideas of what constitutes 'welfare' have changed. Both the pre-Beveridge and the Beveridge schemes concentrated on the provision of a basic minimum. The early scheme thought this primarily a problem for the wage earner, whilst the later insisted that we were all vulnerable and should all be included; but in both it was a secure minimum that was aimed at. This no longer satisfies us.

A weekly sum that is sufficient to enable an unskilled labourer to meet his family obligations without falling into debt is quite inadequate to help a company manager, for example, to pay his way, because his commitments are geared to a different standard. All kinds of extra arrangements have developed to meet this difficulty. There are many voluntary insurance schemes by which men pay an annual premium to provide themselves with a pension when they retire, or a pension for their widows, or to pay for a child's schooling or university course. This is no new thing; it has been done for generations through various friendly societies or profit-making companies. What is new is that now many of these arrangements have become part of the 'conditions of employment' and are organized by employers for the benefit of those in their employment.

Such occupational benefits were originally the exclusive prerogative of the more highly-paid employees—that is, of 'staff' rather than wage earners; but during recent years they have been extended to cover larger and larger groups. It is calculated that almost half of all employees, whatever their grade, are now included in occupational pension schemes; and about two-thirds in sickness schemes which gurantee full pay for so many weeks of absence through illness. In certain of these schemes, the employees pay some contribution towards the occupational fund; in most, however, they are financed solely by the employer and form part of the 'fringe' benefits which are coming to play an ever more important part in wage agreements. In all cases they provide an additional income over and above the statutory benefit received under the national insurance schemes.

The recognition that people live on varying standards when at work and so need different amounts when not at work if they are to feel secure, has led to discussion about altering the national insurance schemes from the present flat-rate type to a comprehensive system of contributions and benefits varying according to the individual's wages. This has already been introduced on a modest scale into Retirement Pensions. Will it become a general feature of the others?

Flexibility or job continuity?

One of the most prized advantages of the white collar worker in the past has been his security of tenure in his work. This does not mean that he could not lose his job; he could and did, but there was much more continuity in his employment than in that of the manual wage earner. In some wage earning occupations one hour's notice of termination was all that was given though in most a week's notice was customary. The higher up one went in non-manual work the longer the period of notice and the more usual for employees to be retained even during periods of bad trade.

The irregularity of employment has long been one of the most hated of all characteristics of manual jobs and now, after two decades of very full employment, most workers are so used to being sought after and regularly employed that any threat to the continuity of a job is bitterly resented. This produces a serious dilemma. On the one hand is the passionate wish for a permanent stake in a job; on the other, a dynamic economy cannot expand unless there is a flexible labour supply. The introduction of new industries and processes, the rapidly changing techniques of production and the large scale changes in the relative demands for different commodities result in constantly changing demands for different kinds of worker. If people refuse to move from where they are no longer needed to where they are, no advantage can be taken of new knowledge to improve production and raise standards of living.

The Contracts of Employment Act, 1963, and the Redundancy Payments Act, 1965, are an attempt to reconcile these two needs. The first gives a worker the right to a certain period of notice or payment in lieu. The second establishes a fund, financed by the contributions of employers, from which workers who have had two years' service with a firm have a legal right to a lump sum compensation on dismissal, related to earnings, age and years of service. This is a long way beyond the concept of security embodied in the first compulsory insurance scheme.

The future

Have all these schemes succeeded in abolishing poverty? If we define poverty as less than the minimum on which people can keep alive, the answer is 'yes'. If we define it as a standard lower than an acceptable minimum for a wealthy community the answer is 'no'. For example, the retirement pension has been constantly increased (by more than enough to compensate for the lower value of money), but yet many old people with no other resources must live very restricted lives if they are to manage on this alone. There is no need for them to do so. The National Assistance Board is ready—even eager—to give them supplementary allowances; but unfortunately a considerable number do not apply for them. This may be due to ignorance of their rights; but more often it is because people who grew up at a time when National Assistance was considered rather shameful, have not adjusted to the new climate of opinion and foolishly refuse to accept what they think of as 'charity'. This raises the question 'What is the best way to deal with this problem?' Should all pensions be increased so as to make sure that no old person is in want even if solely dependent on it? In this case many people would be drawing sums of which they have no need with a resulting much increased burden on the national revenue. And, as the number of old people in the community is rising rapidly, this would mean heavier taxation. Or should we continue the present system of readiness to give generous supplementary allowances wherever there is need, and trust that, as the old ideas die out, people will be ready to apply for them as a matter of course?

An adequate income is the most obvious requirement for every group in a Welfare State but it is not the only one. There are many other questions to which we must find the answers. As people grow older they are often less able to fend for themselves in their own homes. What is needed? Home helps? Meals on Wheels? Special kinds of houses grouped round a centre where assistance can be got in times of ill health or other special circumstances? Residential homes? and if so, what size and how run?

What kinds of towns offer the best kind of life for families? A suburb near to a big city, with all its educational and cultural advantages, but involving long journeys to work? Or a complete but smaller town where people live near their work but have less choice in the other amenities of life? How can we ensure that young people get the kind of education that best suits their capacities? Should all secondary schools be comprehensive? What would be the loss in giving up the old type of grammar school? And how can working people be persuaded to encourage their able children to continue their education as far as their ability takes them?

What is the best way of helping families in the kind of distress which is not caused by lack of income, e.g. to cope with a physically or mentally handicapped member? or a delinquent youngster? or a broken marriage?

It is such questions and considerations as these which we must take into account in our discussion of the future of the Welfare State. It has adjusted itself, by degrees to the changing needs of the community, even if that adjustment has sometimes been tardy, and it has removed, or reduced many hardships that were prevalent a generation ago. But the needs of our society continue to change, and these changes must continue to modify the structure of the Welfare State. We must not regard it as a monument to Booth or Beveridge, as a piece of built-in social history. The Welfare State is not a monument but (as a sculptor would say) a 'mobile'. Its nature is to modify its shape and direction as it responds to the wind of change.

INDEX

For Product Safety Concerns and Information please contact our
EU representative GPSR@taylorandfrancis.com Taylor & Francis
Verlag GmbH, Kaufingerstraße 24, 80331 München, Germany